Morocco. " - - what have we here?
A carrion Death, within whose empty eye
There is a written scroll:"

Act II. Scene VII.

The Copp Clark Literature Series
No. 12

SHAKESPEARE'S

THE MERCHANT OF VENICE

WITH ANNOTATIONS BY

O. J. STEVENSON, M.A., D.Paed.

Professor of English, Ontario Agricultural College, Guelph

ILLUSTRATIONS BY

ELSIE M. STARLING

THE COPP CLARK PUBLISHING CO. LTD.
VANCOUVER   TORONTO   MONTREAL

CONTENTS

INTRODUCTION

The Life of Shakespeare.

William Shakespeare was born in Stratford-on-Avon, in Warwickshire, on April 23rd, 1564. His father, John Shakespeare, was, in early life, a prosperous citizen of Stratford; his mother, Mary Arden, was the daughter of a well-to-do farmer of Warwickshire. Between the ages of seven and fourteen, Shakespeare probably attended the Stratford Grammar School, where, among other things, he received some training in Latin. In the year 1582, before he was nineteen years of age, he married Anne Hathaway, of Shottery, a woman who was some eight years his senior. Two of their children, Susanna and Judith, married, but only one of Shakespeare's grand-children reached maturity, and with her death in 1669 or 1670 the poet's family became extinct.

About the year 1586, Shakespeare left Stratford and went to London, where he appears to have obtained employment in some capacity in connection with the London theatres. About 1588 he began making over old plays, and in 1590 he probably wrote his first original drama. During the next twenty years, from 1590 to 1610, he produced play after play, and there is abundant evidence to show the esteem in which he was held by his contemporaries. In 1594 he was a member of the Earl of Leicester's Company of Players. When the Globe theatre was built in 1599, Shakespeare was one of the chief shareholders, and most of his plays were acted in this theatre.

In the meantime he had begun to acquire property in Stratford. In 1597 he had purchased the fine residence known as New Place, and from this time forward he appears to have looked more and more to Stratford as his home. About the year 1610 or 1611, he left London and returned to Stratford with the apparent intention of living in ease and retirement on the competence which he had accumulated. A few years later, however, his health failed, and he died in April, 1616, in his fifty-second year. He was buried in the chancel of the Church of the Holy Trinity, in Stratford.

Shakespeare's literary career is generally, for the sake of convenience, divided into four periods, according to the character of the plays which he produced:

(*a*) 1588-1594. This is largely a period of apprenticeship. To this period belong, *Love's Labour's Lost*, *Comedy of Errors*, *Richard III.*, and possibly *Romeo and Juliet*.

(b) 1594-1600. During this period most of the great comedies and the English historical plays were produced. To this period belong, *A Midsummer Night's Dream*, *The Merchant of Venice*, *As You Like It*, *Richard II.*, *Henry IV.*, and *Henry V.*

(c) 1600-1606. During this period most of the great tragedies were produced. To this period belong *Julius Cæsar*, *Hamlet*, *Othello*, *King Lear* and *Macbeth*.

(d) 1606-1612. This is a period of later tragedy and of serious comedy. To this period belong, *Antony and Cleopatra*, *Coriolanus*, *Cymbeline*, *The Tempest* and *A Winter's Tale*.

Shakespeare himself took no pains to preserve his plays in permanent form. In all only fifteen of his plays were printed during his lifetime. In 1623, however, seven years after his death, a complete collection of his plays, thirty-six in all, were published in what is known as *The Folio of 1623*.

NOTE.—A folio page is about the size of an ordinary page of foolscap (about 13″ x 8½″), formed by folding the printer's sheet of paper once. When the printer's sheet is divided into four parts, the size of page is known as *quarto*; when divided into eight parts it is *octavo*; when divided into twelve parts it is *duodecimo*. The plays which were printed during Shakespeare's lifetime were published in quarto volumes, as distinguished from the later folios.

The Theatre in Shakespeare's Time.

The first theatre in London was built in 1576, and was known as *The Theatre*. Both this and other theatres which followed, The Curtain, The Globe, Blackfriars, and others, were built outside the city limits in order to escape the restrictions which were placed on the theatre by the Puritans. Most of the theatres were frame structures which were open to the sky, the only roofed part being the stage, or, at most, the raised seats next the walls. The better class of people occupied seats in the boxes overlooking the stage, or sat on stools or reclined on the rushes on the floor of the stage itself. The floor of the pit was merely hard earth, and it was not provided with seats. The admission to the pit was only a penny, and here the rabble crowded together, jostled each other, cracked nuts, ate apples, and laughed and joked and made sport of the actors.

The performance of the play began at three o'clock in the afternoon, and usually lasted two or three hours. The stage was hung with black to indicate tragedy, and with blue to indicate comedy. There was no curtain to mark the opening and closing of the scenes, and beyond a few simple articles of furniture, no scenery of any account was used. At the back of the stage was a sort of gallery or balcony, which served the purpose of an upper room, or any place which was raised above the level of the ordinary scene. A change of place was indicated by a board with the name painted on it, as, London, Venice, Rome, Sardis. A light blue flag was used to indicate a day scene,—a dark flag to indicate a night scene. The women's parts in the play were acted by boys, and women did not appear even among the audience unless they wore masks. It was not until after the Restoration, that movable stage scenery was introduced, and that female parts were acted by women.

The Metre of Shakespeare's Plays.

The plays of Shakespeare are written in blank verse, that is, verse in which the lines do not rhyme. Each line contains five feet, consisting of two syllables each, with the accent falling on the second syllable. This measure is known as *iambic pentameter*.

When we mark the divisions between feet and indicate the accents in a line of poetry, we are said to *scan* it. Where the metre is perfectly regular, the scansion presents no difficulty; but very frequently the poet finds it necessary to vary his metre, either for the sake of avoiding monotony or for the purpose of producing certain special effects. The following are the most important of the variations which occur in the metre of Shakespeare:

(a) Sometimes, especially after a pause, the accent falls upon the first syllable instead of the second, as, for example:

Wo′e to / the ha′nd / that sh′ed / this co′st/ly blo′od!
What ju′dg/ment sh′all / I dre′ad, / do′ing / no wro′ng?

(b) An extra syllable is frequently added, especially at the end of a line, as, for example:

Art th′ou / some g′od, / some a′n/gel o′r / some de′v/il?
It dr′op/peth a′s / the ge′n/tle ra′in / from he′av/en.

(c) Sometimes a foot contains two unaccented syllables, as, for example, in the following lines:

I am ne′v/er m′er/ry wh′en / I he′ar / sweet m′u/sic;
Let me s′ee, / let me s′ee, / was n′ot / the lea′f / turn′d dow′n?

In many cases, however, one of the unaccented syllables is elided, or slurred over in reading, as, for example, in the following:

> Canst tho'u / not m'in/(i)ster t'o / a mi'nd / dise'ased?
> We'll se'nd / Mark A'n/t(o)ny t'o / the Se'n/ate-ho'use.
> Macb'eth / doth m'urder slee'ep, / the i'n/n(o)cent sl'eep.

(*d*) Certain groups of letters which are now pronounced as one syllable, are sometimes pronounced as two syllables in Shakespeare, as, for example, in the following:

> The noble Brutus
> Hath to'ld / you Ca'es/ar wa's ambi'it/i-o'us.
> Misli'ke / me n'ot / for m'y / comple'x/i-o'n.

(*e*) It frequently happens that among the accented syllables in a line of poetry some have a stronger stress than others; and in order to scan a line, it is sometimes necessary to accent words which according to the sense have no stress, as, for example, in the case of the italicized words in the following:

> Throw phy's/ic *to'* / the do'gs; / I'll no'ne / of i't!
> There *i's* / a ti'de / in *th'e* / affa'irs / of me'n.

Rhyme is used by Shakespeare chiefly for the purpose of giving emphasis to those lines in which the speaker expresses a purpose or decision, and it very frequently marks the close of a scene. Shakespeare used rhyme much more freely in his earlier than in his later plays.

Prose. Shakespeare makes use of prose in his plays wherever the characters belong to a lower level of society, as, for example, the citizens in *Julius Cæsar*, the porter in *Macbeth*, and Lancelot Gobbo, the clown, in *The Merchant of Venice*. Prose is also used in letters, as, for example, that of Bellario in *The Merchant of Venice*, and for rhetorical speeches, as in the case of the paper of Artemidorus and the oration of Brutus in *Julius Cæsar*. Sometimes also, prose is used for the purpose of producing a special dramatic effect, as in the case of Casca's assumed bluntness of manner in *Julius Cæsar;* and in the scene in *The Merchant of Venice* where Shylock is "tortured" by Tubal; and in the sleep-walking scene in *Macbeth*.

THE MERCHANT OF VENICE

Date of the Play.

The Merchant of Venice was first published by a printer named Roberts, in a quarto edition, in the year 1600. But we know that it was written as early as 1598, for it is entered in the *Stationers' Register* (similar to our copyright registration) in July of that year; and in a book called *Palladis Tamia* or *Wit's Treasury*, written by one Francis Meres, and published in September, 1598, it is also mentioned. There are some critics who argue that it must have been written as early as 1594; but the evidence for this date is very slight, and in all probability it was produced in the year 1596 or 1597.

Sources of the Plot.

The Merchant of Venice contains two main stories—the bond story and the caskets story; and growing out of these are two minor stories—the elopement of Lorenzo and Jessica and the episode of the rings. The story of the pound of flesh and the story of the caskets are both very old, and they appear in various forms in different collections of mediæval tales and romances. It appears certain, however, that Shakespeare obtained the material for the bond story, including the Ring's Episode, from a collection of tales entitled *Il Pecorone*, compiled by an Italian named Ser Giovanni Fiorentino and published in 1558. The material for the caskets story he obtained from a collection of mediæval tales called *Gesta Romanorum* (The Deeds of the Romans), which was well known in Shakespeare's day. Nothing definite is known as to where Shakespeare obtained the material for the story of Lorenzo and Jessica. It may be, however, that the idea was suggested to him by the play entitled *The Jew of Malta* written by his contemporary, Christopher Marlowe, or by an Italian tale written during the preceding century which contains much the same story.

Shakespeare as a rule did not invent much of the material which he used in the construction of his plots. He simply took the material which he found ready at hand and remoulded it in dramatic form. In the case of *The Merchant of Venice* he used the bond story in *Il Pecorone* as the basis of his plot. Then in place of the test to which the lover in the Italian story is subjected he substituted the story of the caskets; and into these combined stories he wove the romance of Lorenzo and Jessica. The outlines of the stories are borrowed; but the language, the sentiments, the characters, and the wonderful skill with which the stories are woven into one, are all Shakespeare's own.

The Title of the Play.

There is no doubt that in giving the title *The Merchant of Venice* to the play, Shakespeare did not intend merely to name the play after Antonio; for, as a matter of fact, Antonio is not so striking a character as either Shylock or Bassanio. The title is appropriate because it suggests the conditions which form the background of the plot as a whole. It was because Antonio was a rich merchant and occupied a position of influence on the Rialto that he came into contact with Shylock; and it was in part because he was a rich merchant that Bassanio was able to borrow from him. It was, moreover, because he was a "merchant of Venice,"—one whose ventures were "squandered abroad"—that it was possible for him to lose all his wealth at sea. In depicting the character of Antonio the dramatist has, to be sure, made much of his generous nature and his loyal friendship for Bassanio, but it is in reality because the plot turns upon the position and fortunes of "the merchant of Venice" that the play is named after him.

"The Merchant of Venice" as a Comedy.

When we speak of a Comedy we usually have in mind the kind of play that is cheerful in tone and that has a happy ending. But as a matter of fact the tone and the ending are in themselves always dependent upon other conditions in the play. In comedy as in tragedy the plot consists in the development of some difficulty which has to be overcome. If the hero or heroine is able to solve the problem, or overcome the difficulty, the play ends happily, and usually in such cases the whole tone of the play is cheerful. To a play of this kind we give the name of comedy. But if on the other hand, the hero or heroine is unable to meet the difficulty successfully, and is himself overcome by it, the play becomes a tragedy. *The Merchant of Venice* contains material for a great tragedy. Let us suppose, for instance, that Bassanio had been so lacking in experience and judgment as to choose the wrong casket: Portia in that case could never have gone to the assistance of Antonio. And, furthermore, if Portia herself had been unable to solve the problem of the bond, which had apparently baffled everyone else, Antonio would have been sacrificed and Shylock would have triumphed. It is because in these two crises in the play Bassanio and Portia in turn prove equal to the difficulty that presents itself, that the play is cheerful in tone and ends happily. The dramatist has at the same time, however, introduced comic elements,—the buffoonery of Launcelot, the wit of Portia, the humour of the Rings' Episode,—that fall in with the prevailing tone of the play. If the play were transformed into a tragedy, a different setting must be provided for the great crises in the play.

The Structure of the Play.

In *The Merchant of Venice* Shakespeare has combined two main stories, the story of the bond and the story of the caskets,—and two minor stories,—the Elopement of Lorenzo and Jessica and the Rings' Episode. And although each of these four stories has a distinct interest of its own, so perfectly have they been interwoven that no one of the stories is in itself independent of the others, and each story contributes in its own way to the unity of the plot.

The two main stories, the bond story and the caskets story, grow out of Bassanio's broken fortunes. In order to repair his loss of fortune he proposes to make suit to the wealthy Portia, with whom it happens he is really in love; but before he can present himself as a suitor he must have money. Hence the necessity of the bond by means of which Antonio borrows money of Shylock. These two stories alternately occupy the interest of the audience during the first half of the play; and both reach their crisis in the middle of the third Act, when simultaneously with the success of Bassanio comes the news that Antonio's bond is forfeit.

In the meantime, however, the dramatist has made use of special means to maintain a close connection between the two stories. To begin with, the clown, Launcelot Gobbo, who has been employed by Shylock, enters the service of Bassanio, and Shylock is glad to part with him because he will help to waste Bassanio's borrowed purse. At the same time, too, Shylock has been "bid forth to supper" by Bassanio, and he goes in hate to feed upon the prodigal Christian. Lorenzo, the guest of Bassanio, has in the meantime fallen in love with Shylock's daughter Jessica; and the intrigue of the lovers is a means of connecting the two stories. And finally the flight of Jessica with a Christian and with a friend of Bassanio, and her theft of ducats and jewels, has the effect of enraging Shylock still further against Antonio, so as to make it certain that if the bond should fall due, he will exact the forfeiture.

The crises of the two stories meet, as we have seen, in the centre of the play; and as a result of the good judgment of Bassanio the problem of the caskets is successfully solved. The latter half of the play is then devoted mainly to the solution of the problem which the bond story presents. And now just as in the first half of the play Bassanio's need of money has helped to bring about the crisis in the affairs of Antonio,—so in the second half of the play his success in the choice of the caskets proves to be the means by which Antonio is rescued from his perilous position. Portia, now having the interests of Bassanio at heart, devises and carries out the plan by which Shylock is cheated of his revenge. At the same time, in order to preserve the balance of the play, Lorenzo and Jessica and Launcelot are transferred from Venice to Belmont, and their arrival just at the opportune time makes it easier for Portia to carry out her plans. At the close of the Trial Scene, furthermore, the audience are reconciled all the more readily to the punishment that is meted out to Shylock, when it is remembered that Lorenzo and Jessica are to benefit by the deed of gift which Shylock is forced to draw up in their favour. The Rings' Episode with which the play concludes is not so essential to the main plot as the Jessica story; but it serves to relieve the intense strain of the latter half of the play: and besides as the play closes it furnishes an indisputable proof to Bassanio and Gratiano that Portia and Nerissa were in reality judge and clerk at the trial.

To sum up, then, we have in the first half of the play the development of the caskets story and the bond story, both growing out of Bassanio's loss of fortune; and these stories are closely connected, not only by the common interests of Bassanio and Antonio, but by the subordinate incidents in the play, and in particular by the story of Lorenzo and Jessica. The two main stories reach their crisis in the middle of the play; and the success of Bassanio in the choice of the caskets brings with it also a solution of the difficulty in the bond story, inasmuch as it makes it possible for Portia to act as judge at the trial of Antonio. The arrival of Lorenzo and Jessica at Belmont makes it easier for Portia to carry out her plan; and at the same time Lorenzo and Jessica are, as it were, a sort of compensation for Shylock when sentence is pronounced upon him at the close of the trial. The Rings' Episode with which the story concludes, provides a happy ending for the play, and at the same time furnishes proof that Portia and Nerissa have indeed been present as judge and clerk respectively at the trial of Antonio.

Sources of Interest in the Play.

In *The Merchant of Venice*, as in other dramas, the main sources of interest lie in the development of plot and the portrayal of character. But aside from these general sources of interest the dramatist has used special means to arouse and hold the attention of the audience.

Unusual Situations and Incidents. In the first place, many of the situations or incidents in the play are in themselves so unusual or so picturesque as to awaken and hold the interest. To begin with, the bargain between Antonio and Shylock in which a pound of flesh is named as the forfeiture is sufficiently strange to challenge the attention. In the Second Act the masque forms a picturesque setting for the elopement of Lorenzo and Jessica. Nothing could be more romantic than the method by which Portia is to be won, and the choice of the caskets is made all the more striking by the fact that one of the suitors is "a tawnie Moor" and another a broken-down

Spanish prince. In the Trial Scene besides the strange nature of the suit, there is an added interest in the fact that Portia is the judge and that the wit of this "wise young judge" is matched against the cunning of Shylock. And, finally, the moonlight scene in Portia's grounds forms a picturesque conclusion to the series of unusual situations in the play.

Dramatic Irony. When the words or actions of a character in the play have for the audience a significance the opposite of that which is intended, this double significance constitutes dramatic irony. In *The Merchant of Venice* a number of the situations are in themselves ironical. The wealthy Antonio borrowing from his enemy Shylock, the deliberate Arragon choosing the casket with a death's head, Shylock insisting on "the very words" of the bond, these and other incidents in the play have a significance for the audience which they have not for the actors themselves, and in so far they are ironical. On two different occasions in the play this element of irony creates a humorous situation. In the Trial Scene both Bassanio and Gratiano swear that they would willingly sacrifice their wives in order to deliver Antonio; and after the return to Belmont Gratiano adds to the humour of the situation by his unconscious description of Nerissa as "a prating boy" and "a little scrubbed boy no higher than thyself."

Nemesis. In the course of any drama the author must see that the good qualities of his heroes are rewarded, and that the mistakes or crimes of which they are guilty are punished. Sometimes under certain conditions we feel that the punishment is peculiarly suited to the crime, and to this form of retributive justice we give the name of *Nemesis*. In *The Merchant of Venice* the element of nemesis appears in its most striking form in the case of Antonio and of Shylock respectively. In spite of the kindness and generosity of Antonio, the fact remains that he had treated Shylock unjustly: and furthermore, when he comes to borrow money of Shylock, we cannot help feeling that he is over-confident, and that in signing the bond he is running too great a risk. We are not surprised then when nemesis overtakes him, and in the "gaoler scene" in Act III. we feel that his humiliation is complete. But, on the other hand, Antonio's warm-hearted generosity has won for him the admiration and affection of his friends: and the audience feel that it is only a matter of justice that some compensation should be made to him for all his losses and misfortunes. We know that he is to have one half of Shylock's goods in use until his death, and the audience is not ill-pleased to learn of the good news which Portia has in store for him at the close of the play, when she bids him unseal the letter announcing that three of his argosies have safely arrived in harbour.

In the case of Shylock, nemesis takes on a more complicated form. We know that Shylock had some good qualities,— among others his affection for his daughter and for his dead wife Leah; but to an Elizabethan audience the good elements in his character were far outweighed by his evil qualities,—his miserliness, his hatred of the Christians, and his desire for revenge upon Antonio. It was, then only a form of nemesis, a judgment by which he was justly overtaken, when his own daughter forsook him and fled with a Christian, when he was robbed of money and jewels, and when finally he himself was forced to turn Christian and to leave the one half his goods in use to his hated enemy Antonio. But it is in the Trial Scene that the spirit of nemesis shows itself in its most striking form. Shylock will listen to no prayers for mercy: he will not accept the offer of thrice the money, but stands for justice and his bond. To all appeals on behalf of Antonio he returns the answer, "I cannot find it: it is not in the bond." And when at length his own weapons—his very words indeed,—are turned against him, it seems as if the judgment were peculiarly appropriate to the occasion.

The Choice of the Caskets.

The comparison of the three suitors in *The Merchant of Venice* so as to show their characters and the motives which governed them in the choice of the caskets, is one of the chief elements of interest in the study of the play. In Act I., Scene II., we are told that the choice of the caskets is not a mere lottery, but the means devised by a wise and virtuous father to make certain that his daughter will be chosen only by the man who truly loves her. In order to make sure that no one will offer to choose the caskets unless he is willing to risk everything on the choice, the suitors are required to take an oath that if they fail they will never afterward speak to lady in way of marriage. As a result of this imposition, this "parcel of wooers," described by Portia in Scene II., have decided to return home. But just as their decision is announced, a messenger brings word of the arrival of the Prince of Morocco.

Can you imagine the scene? Morocco is dark-skinned—"with the complexion of a devil,"—but dressed with a magnificence becoming a southern prince, and with a splendid retinue. He is vain, but his vanity is not wholly displeasing, because it is frank and open, and because it finds expression in his gallantry towards Portia. He swears "by his love"; Portia is his "gentle queen"; if he misses her he will "die with grieving," and if he wins he will be the most "blest among men;" and when he loses, he bows himself out of her presence with "too grieved a heart to take a tedious leave."

When he comes at length to make his choice of the caskets, it is partly his vanity, and partly his gallantry, that proves his undoing. He cannot think that lead contains "her heavenly picture." And silver is not rich enough for Portia, although the inscription on the silver casket tempts him and makes him pause a moment to recount his own deservings. But it is the golden casket that appeals most strongly to his vanity. "What many men desire"—this is the flame and Morocco is the moth! What every one wishes, the vain, boastful, showy, gallant Morocco must have, and he grows eloquent over the fancied picture of the suitors from "the four corners of the earth," over whom he, Morocco, will triumph. He chooses,—and Portia's wise father is vindicated. It is selfish vanity rather than love for Portia that leads him to choose as he does; and when Portia, who sees through his shallow boastfulness, takes leave of him, there is no doubt a double meaning in her ironical farewell:

> "A gentle riddance! Draw the curtains, Go!
> Let all of his *complexion* choose me so!"

The Prince of Arragon is a suitor of a different type,—a Spanish grandee, who seeks to repair his broken fortunes by marriage with Portia. It is evident that in his conversation with Portia, he makes no effort to please her. He makes no recital of his virtues, and shows nothing of the open gallantry of Morocco. He deliberately repeats the conditions of his oath so as to be sure there is no mistake and at once sets himself to choose. Perhaps in giving this Spanish prince the name of Arragon, Shakespeare meant to give the audience a hint of his proud and *arrogant* character, which is shown in his speech. He dismisses the leaden casket in a word, as beneath his dignity; and the inscription, "who chooseth me must give and hazard all he hath"; does not appeal to him, for it is not a part of his selfish nature to give or hazard for others. The inscription on the golden casket moves him to an expression of scorn for the "many men,"— "the fool multitude," the "common spirits," and "barbarous multitudes," whom he held in contempt. But the silver casket with its bait of *deserts* appeals at once to his selfish pride, and he is moved to eloquence at the thought of his own deservings. His speech on *"merit"* has a splendid ring about it, even if the sentiment is commonplace, until we discover that his idea of "merit" is not that of character, but merely that of noble birth. If he, Arragon, were allowed to set things right, his first task would be to pull down the "low peasantry" who have risen by real merit, and set up "the true seed of honour"—who but the proud Arragon himself?—in their place. And so Arragon chooses the silver casket, and in so doing he too makes it clear that it is not Portia that he worships, but his selfish idea of his own deserts.

Arragon had taken an oath that if he should fail, he would, "without more speech" immediately be gone; but when he chooses wrongly he at once begins to find fault with the conditions:

> "Did I deserve no more than a fool's head?
> Are my deserts no better?"

This calls forth a rebuke from Portia, who reminds him that he who makes a mistake is not a fit person to sit in judgment upon his own misfortunes. And when he takes his leave, her opinion of his "merits" is shown by her stinging comment:

> "O, these *deliberate* fools! When they do choose,
> They have the wisdom by their wit to lose."

Bassanio makes his choice under more favourable circumstances than either Morocco or Arragon. He had visited Portia before, while her father was still alive, and from her eyes, even then, he "did receive fair speechless messages." To Nerissa, who saw him then, "he of all men was the best deserving a fair lady," and Portia, who remembers him well, agrees that he is worthy of Nerissa's praise. The messenger whom he send before, to announce his approach, brings "gifts of rich value;" and we know that Bassanio himself was prepared "to hold a rival place," in outward show, with other suitors. We are told that Bassanio was a welcome suitor, and Portia, as far as her womanly modesty will permit, leaves him in no doubt as to her own anxiety that he will choose aright.

Bassanio was from the outset less likely than either Morocco or Arragon, to be tempted by the "outward shows" of the gold and silver caskets. He was "a soldier and a scholar;" and his own past experience in which he had "disabled his estate," had no doubt put him in a position to form sound judgments as to the real values of external appearances.

This lesson had, indeed, been brought home to him by his preparation for this very event; for when Shylock had attempted to justify himself by quoting from Scripture, Antonio had warned Bassanio especially, that outside appearances were not to be trusted:

> "Mark you this, Bassanio,
> The devil can cite Scripture for his purpose.
> An evil soul, producing holy witness,
> Is like a villain with a smiling cheek;
> A goodly apple rotten at the heart,
> O, what a goodly outside falsehood hath."

The song that is sung while Bassanio is choosing, helps to confirm the judgment at which he has already arrived. "What of love?" says the singer; "Is it a thing of the heart or of the head?" If it is a thing of the head only, merely dependent upon outward beauty which pleases the eyes, it cannot live. "So may the outward shows be least themselves," comments Bassanio; "The world is still deceived with ornament." It cannot be said that the song gave Bassanio any real hint as to which casket he should choose; for to either Morocco or Arragon the words of the song would have meant nothing. It is only because the song falls in with his own thoughts that it calls forth a response from Bassanio.

And so he chooses the leaden casket. He is a soldier, and the leaden casket threatens. He is both a scholar and a man of the world and he has learned by experience that ornament is deceptive. But, more than all, he loves Portia truly, and the leaden casket calls upon him to "give" for her sake, while the gold and silver tempt him with offers of "gain." When Portia, in the early part of the story, complained because she was unable "to choose one nor refuse none," Nerissa comforted her with the reflection that the caskets would "never be chosen rightly, but by one who should rightly love." When Bassanio chose the leaden casket, Nerissa's prediction came true.

The Important Characters in "The Merchant of Venice."

Antonio. Although the bond story arises out of the relations of Antonio to Shylock and Bassanio, yet Antonio himself does not in person play an important part in *The Merchant of Venice*; and his character as presented in the play is not difficult to analyse or to understand. From his relations with Shylock it appears that he is a merchant of influence on the Rialto; and throughout the play we are given the impression that he possesses great wealth. His enmity towards Shylock seems to have grown wholly out of the fact that Shylock was a usurer, and that he oppressed those who came into his power. But Antonio in showing his contempt for Shylock had apparently heaped upon him personal indignities which aroused his bitter hatred. And when Shylock complains of his treatment Antonio replies:

> "I am as like to call thee so (dog) again,
> To spit on thee again, to spurn thee too."

Besides showing this spirit of intolerance towards Shylock, Antonio is over-confident as to his own fortunes; and this blind confidence, as we have seen, brings with it its own nemesis.

Aside from his relations towards Shylock, Antonio is best judged by the estimation in which he is held by his friends. Salarino says of him, "a kinder gentleman treads not the earth." Bassanio describes him as "the best conditioned and unwearied spirit in doing courtesies," and Lorenzo in speaking to Portia regarding him assures her that he is one to whom she might be proud to send relief. In the beginning of the play he is represented as being overcome by an unaccountable sadness, and his mood throughout the drama is naturally not a cheerful one; but in his friendship for Bassanio he gives evidence of a self-sacrificing generosity which in itself justifies the admiration and affection of his friends.

Portia. It would be difficult to give a better summary of the qualities of Portia than that uttered by Bassanio when he describes her as "fair, and fairer than that word, of wondrous virtues." But to understand fully what these "wondrous virtues" are, it will be necessary to see Portia herself as she appears in the different scenes in the play. In the conversation with Nerissa (Act I., Scene II.), in which the different suitors are described, it is her keenness of intellect, and the play of wit and humour, that attracts us most strongly; but at the same time beneath this playful exterior we feel that there is an undercurrent of seriousness, and that her vivacity in reality covers up her real feelings of anxiety concerning the conditions of her father's will. In the scenes in which Morocco and Arragon make their choice of the caskets we have a further illustration of Portia's attitude towards her unwelcome suitors, in the case of Morocco an amused tolerance, which gives way to genuine relief when he takes his departure; and in the case of Arragon an ill-concealed contempt, which finds its expression at length in biting sarcasm. But with Bassanio it is different. She had already seen him in her father's time and the "fair speechless messages" in her eyes were in themselves a sufficient proof of her feelings towards him. When he comes as a suitor there is the inevitable struggle between love and modesty in which both feelings alternately find expression; and throughout the scene all the womanly qualities in her nature, qualities of heart rather than of intellect, are revealed. In Act IV. her conduct of the Trial Scene shows not only keenness of intellect but self-control and firmness of will; and these qualities of mind stand out all the more clearly because they form a contrast to the girlish playfulness which she displays both in her preparation for her **journey to Venice and in her conversation with Bassanio at**

the close of the trial. When she returns again to Belmont she appears for the moment in a reflective mood. Perhaps she has been subdued by the events of the day, for the light of the candle shining in the distance reminds her of 'a good deed in a naughty world,' or perhaps she too has fallen under the spell of the music and the moonlight. But when Bassanio returns, her light-hearted raillery shows that she is the same Portia as of old, whose gaiety and vivacity of spirit are not least among "the wondrous virtues" which Bassanio had foretold.

> "A perfect woman, nobly planned
>   To warn, to comfort, and command;
> And yet a spirit still and bright
>   With something of an angel light."

Shylock. In the picture which Shakespeare draws of Shylock he has represented him, in the main, as having the traditional qualities of the Jewish money-lender,—on the one hand a passion for his own race and religion, and on the other, a mean and sordid way of living which is the result of his miserly disposition. But while these are the outstanding features in Shylock's character, Shakespeare has so portrayed them that they seem to be natural qualities belonging to a real human being, with human weaknesses and human passions, rather than either a type or a caricature of a real individual.

We first meet Shylock in the Borrowing Scene, in circumstances that cannot fail to bring out his long-standing, racial and personal prejudices. His hated enemy Antonio has come to him to borrow three thousand ducats, and Shylock sees in this occasion the opportunity of satisfying "the ancient grudge" which he bears Antonio. The causes of that grudge are made plain to the audience in the soliloquy of Shylock at the moment when Bassanio goes forward to greet Antonio:

> "I hate him for he is a Christian,
>   But more for that in low simplicity
> He lends out money gratis and brings down
>   The rate of usance here with us in Venice.
>
> .   .   .   .
>
> He hates our sacred nation, and he rails,
>   Even there whose merchants most do congregate,
> On me, my bargains and my well-won thrift,
>   Which he calls interest."

At the beginning of the scene it is evident that Shylock has no definite idea of how he can turn this opportunity to advantage; and when Antonio urges his request, Shylock reproaches him with the indignities which he has suffered from Antonio in the past. It is evidently Antonio's reply,

> "If thou wilt lend this money, lend it not
> As to thy friends; *for when did friendship take
> A breed of barren metal of his friend?*"

that gives Shylock the idea of taking interest in the form of a pound of flesh: for at once his whole tone changes and he attempts to disarm the suspicion of Antonio and Bassanio by speaking of the bond as a piece of "merry sport," and by assuring them that he wishes to buy the friendship of Antonio by lending him the money free of interest.

In the scenes in which Shylock next appears in the play, we are given some insight into the character of his home life,— and we are left to judge how hard and sordid that home life must be. Jessica in speaking of her home says, "Our house is hell"; and Launcelot declares that he is famished in Shylock's service. When Shylock is about to set forth for supper, the directions which he gives to Jessica show how dull and narrow is the life which he forces her to lead; and his parting threat, "Perhaps I will return immediately," shows the atmosphere of mean suspicion in which his household lives.

In the beginning of Act III. we see Shylock again after he has learned of Jessica's elopement with Lorenzo, and just at the moment when further news is brought regarding Antonio's misfortunes. There is little need to analyse this scene to show the effect of these two incidents in arousing the passions of Shylock,—his hatred of the Christians, his grief over his losses, his eagerness for revenge, mingled with his blind fury at the flight of his daughter and his despair when he learns of the loss of his turquoise which had been given him by his dead wife Leah. It is probable that when Shylock first proposed the bond he intended only to humiliate Antonio; but he is goaded by these losses as well as by the taunts of his enemies, to a frenzy which can be satisfied only by the life of Antonio. And Shakespeare has taken care to show that in this passion for revenge Shylock is only human. There are few passages in the play as fine as that which Shakespeare puts into the mouth of Shylock in this scene in vindication of the human passions of the Jew.

This scene provides an explanation for Shylock's conduct in the remainder of the play. We are not surprised that he refuses Antonio's plea for mercy, in the Gaoler Scene; and in the Trial Scene his replies to the pleadings of the Duke and Portia alike are an assertion of his individual rights, for which his enemies in the court-room could with difficulty find an answer. Supposing it had been possible for the dramatist to represent Shylock as taking a middle course involving merely the humiliation of Antonio without an attempt upon his life, our sympathies would, on the whole, have been with the Jew. It is because his blind hatred leads him to extremes of "hellish cruelty" that he fails to hold the sympathy of the audience. Even as it is, at the close of the Trial Scene the audience are left with a feeling of half pity for him as he gropes his way out of the court-room to the lonely life of his cheerless and deserted home.

Jessica. In order that the audience may look with favour upon Jessica it is necessary that Shakespeare should represent her as being out of sympathy with Shylock and his mode of living. Shylock is a miser; Jessica, on the other hand, spends money freely. She gives Launcelot a ducat for carrying a message to Lorenzo. She gilds herself with ducats upon leaving her father's house and squanders them recklessly. Shylock lives meanly; Jessica complains that their house is hell, and is thankful that though she is a daughter to his blood she is not to his manners. Shylock is a Jew, but Jessica, on the other hand, is quite content to forsake the Jewish faith and become a Christian. But even in the effort to represent Jessica as being different from Shylock, the dramatist is in danger of alienating our sympathies from her upon another score: for no matter how mean and miserly Shylock may be, it is difficult to justify Jessica's conduct towards him. Shakespeare has attempted to meet this difficulty partially by putting into the mouth of Jessica a half apology for her conduct (Act II., Scene III., ll. 14-15); and Shylock's very miserliness seems to form a sort of excuse for robbing him. But the chief thing upon which Shakespeare relies for this dramatic justification is the personal attractiveness of Jessica herself. Her beauty appeals to the artistic beauty-loving Lorenzo, and calls forth an exclamation of admiration from Gratiano. In the Elopement Scene she shows a modesty that well becomes her; and in the other scenes in which she appears, she shows that she is by no means lacking in wit and intelligence. It is she, not Lorenzo, who plans the details of the elopement, and in the moonlight scene in Act V. she proves herself to be a match for Lorenzo in the contest of wits in which the lovers engage. And even if there were no sufficient dramatic justification for her conduct toward Shylock it must not be forgotten that the audience is likely to be indulgent towards her because of the romantic part she plays in the story. To lovers in the drama much can be forgiven.

Lorenzo is, for obvious reasons, of less dramatic importance in the play than Jessica. As far as we have an opportunity to judge of his character he is of a dreamy meditative nature, to whom the beauty of the music and the moonlight night at Portia's home strongly appeals. He is of a reflective turn of mind, as we judge from his conversation with Jessica, and is at the same time not without a sense of humour. But, true to his type, he is unthrifty, and he frankly confesses that the good news which Nerissa has brought to himself and Jessica from Venice comes to them like manna to starved people.

Gratiano. The chief characteristics of Gratiano that make him a favourite character in the play are his high spirits and sense of humour. Bassanio, it is true, says of him that he "speaks an infinite deal of nothing, more than any man in all Venice," and on at least two occasions in the play he delivers a set speech apparently just for the pleasure of talking. But his high spirits are infectious, and even if he is "too wild, too rude and bold of voice" on certain occasions, his boisterous mirth, nevertheless, adds greatly to our enjoyment of the play.

Nerissa forms a foil for Portia, just as Gratiano does for Bassanio. In her conversation with Portia in the beginning of the play she shows that she is vivacious and quick-witted. Portia, indeed, treats her rather as a friend and confidant than as her waiting-maid. Nerissa, on the other hand, enters into the spirit of all Portia's plans and shares in the fun which is created by the Rings' Episode in the last Act of the play.

Salarino and Salanio. Of these two characters all that can be said is that they are lively talkative "gossips," who are keenly interested in the fortunes of Antonio and Bassanio. They do not take any important part in the action, but their gossip helps to show the turn that events are taking and we are able to judge by their feelings how the dramatist wishes the audience to view the incidents in the play.

Launcelot Gobbo does not belong to the class of professional jesters. He is merely a serving-man who is a mixture of ignorance and buffoonery. His humour consists chiefly in his misuse of words and his fondness for using high-sounding expressions which have little or no meaning. Much of the amusement which the audience derives from Launcelot depends upon the buffoonery of the actor, who helps out Launcelot's words by gestures and actions which are equally ludicrous.

Time Analysis.

The action of *The Merchant of Venice* covers a period of a little over three months. In the first scene Antonio sends Bassanio out to borrow the money which he requires in order to prosecute his suit with Portia. Bassanio, no doubt, goes at once to Shylock, and at the close of the First Act the bond is signed. About the middle of Act III. we learn that the three months have expired, and that the bond has become forfeit. Bassanio at once sets out for Venice, and Portia follows on the same day. The trial, no doubt, takes place on the day following. Bassanio remains over night at Antonio's house, and in the meantime Portia and Nerissa make their way leisurely homeward. The following evening they arrive at Belmont.

It is evident that the chief difficulty regarding the time element in the play lies in the necessity of making the audience feel that three months have actually passed between the time when the bond is signed in Act I., and the time when it falls due in Act III. In order to give the impression of the passage of time, Shakespeare employs two devices. In the first place he engages the attention of the audience by a series of incidents, each of which in itself occupies some time. Launcelot leaves the service of Shylock to enter the service of Bassanio. Bassanio in the meantime is busied with preparations for his journey, and among other things he plans a feast for his friends. Lorenzo and his companions make arrangements for a masque, under cover of which Jessica leaves her father's house. Bassanio sets sail, and in the meantime Shylock raises an outcry regarding his losses. At the same time that these incidents are going forward in Venice, Morocco and Arragon successively make their choice of the caskets, and Bassanio's arrival at Belmont is announced. All these details, spread, as they are, over nine different scenes in Act II., help to suggest the passage of time.

The second device which Shakespeare employs in order to give the impression that time is passing is the use of what is known as *double time*. That is to say, he speaks of coming events as near at hand and of past events as if they had taken place a considerable time before. In Act II., Scene I., for instance, he gives us the impression that Bassanio has been busy for some time in making preparations to set out for Belmont, and the reference to the feast which he intends to give to his "best esteemed acquaintance," suggests that the preparations are now nearly complete. In Scene VIII. the account which Salarino and Salanio give of the departure of Bassanio, and of Shylock's rage, implies that some time has elapsed since these events have taken place; and there is also a suggestion in this scene that the time is fast approaching when Antonio's bond will become forfeit. Finally in Act III., Scene I., the news which Tubal brings regarding Lorenzo and Jessica again helps to give the impression that a further period of time has elapsed: and at the same time we are definitely told that it is now within a fortnight of the time when the bond will fall due. In the following scene, Salerio arrives at Belmont with a letter from Antonio announcing that the bond has become forfeit; but the audience has been gradually prepared for the ill-news and when the announcement is made, it causes little surprise.

THE DUKE OF VENICE.
THE PRINCE OF MOROCCO, } suitors to Portia.
THE PRINCE OF ARRAGON,
ANTONIO, a Merchant of Venice.
BASSANIO, his friend, suitor likewise to Portia.
SALANIO,
SALARINO,
GRATIANO, } friends to Antonio and Bassanio.
SALERIO,
LORENZO, in love with Jessica.
SHYLOCK, a rich Jew.
TUBAL, a Jew, his friend.
LAUNCELOT GOBBO, the clown, servant to Shylock.
OLD GOBBO, father to Launcelot.
LEONARDO, servant to Bassanio.
BALTHASAR,
STEPHANO, } servants to Portia.
PORTIA, a rich heiress.
NERISSA, her waiting-maid.
JESSICA, daughter to Shylock.

Magnificoes of Venice, Officers of the Court of Justice, Gaoler,
Servants to Portia, and other Attendants.

SCENE:—*Partly at Venice, and partly at Belmont, the seat of Portia.
on the Continent.*

THE MERCHANT OF VENICE

ACT I

SCENE I. *Venice. A street.*

Enter ANTONIO, SALARINO, *and* SALANIO.

Antonio. In sooth, I know not why I am so sad:
It wearies me; you say it wearies you;
But how I caught it, found it, or came by it,
What stuff 'tis made of, whereof it is born,
I am to learn;
And such a want-wit sadness makes of me
That I have much ado to know myself.

   Salarino. Your mind is tossing on the ocean;
There, where your argosies with portly sail,
Like signiors and rich burghers on the flood,   10
Or, as it were, the pageants of the sea,
Do overpeer the petty traffickers,
That curtsy to them, do them reverence,
As they fly by them with their woven wings.

   Salanio. Believe me, sir, had I such venture forth,
The better part of my affections would
Be with my hopes abroad. I should be still
Plucking the grass, to know where sits the wind,
Peering in maps for ports and piers and roads;
And every object that might make me fear   20
Misfortune to my ventures out of doubt
Would make me sad.

Salarino.   My wind cooling my broth
Would blow me to an ague, when I thought
What harm a wind too great at sea might do.
I should not see the sandy hour-glass run.
But I should think of shallows and of flats,
And see my wealthy Andrew dock'd in sand,
Vailing her high-top lower than her ribs
To kiss her burial.   Should I go to church
And see the holy edifice of stone,   30
And not bethink me straight of dangerous rocks,
Which touching but my gentle vessel's side,
Would scatter all her spices on the stream,
Enrobe the roaring waters with my silks,
And, in a word, but even now worth this,
And now worth nothing?   Shall I have the thought
To think on this, and shall I lack the thought
That such a thing bechanced would make me sad?
But tell not me; I know, Antonio
Is sad to think upon his merchandise.   40

Antonio.   Believe me, no: I thank my fortune for it,
My ventures are not in one bottom trusted,
Nor to one place; nor is my whole estate
Upon the fortune of this present year;
Therefore my merchandise makes me not sad.

Salarino.   Why, then you are in love.

Antonio.   Fie, fie!

Salar.   Not in love neither?   Then let us say you are
          sad,
Because you are not merry; and 'twere as easy   50
For you to laugh and leap and say you are merry,
Because you are not sad.   Now, by two-headed Janus,
Nature hath framed strange fellows in her time:

Some that will evermore peep through their eyes
And laugh like parrots at a bag-piper,
And other of such vinegar aspect
That they'll not show their teeth in way of smile,
Though Nestor swear the jest be laughable.

Enter BASSANIO, LORENZO, *and* GRATIANO.

Salanio.   Here comes Bassanio, your most noble
  kinsman,   60
Gratiano and Lorenzo.   Fare ye well;
We leave you now with better company.
 Salar.   I would have stay'd till I had made you merry,
If worthier friends had not prevented me.
 Antonio.   Your worth is very dear in my regard.
I take it, your own business calls on you
And you embrace the occasion to depart.
 Salarino.   Good morrow, my good lords.
 Bass.   Good signiors both, when shall we laugh? say,
  when?   70
You grow exceeding strange: must it be so?
 Salarino.   We'll make our leisures to attend on yours.

       [*Exeunt Salarino and Salanio.*

 Lor.   My Lord Bassanio, since you have found Antonio,
We two will leave you; but at dinner-time,
I pray you, have in mind where we must meet.
 Bassanio.   I will not fail you.
 Gratiano.   You look not well, Signior Antonio;
You have too much respect upon the world:
They lose it that do buy it with much care:
Believe me, you are marvellously changed.   80
 Antonio.   I hold the world but as the world, Gratiano;
A stage where every man must play a part,
And mine a sad one

Gratiano.   Let me play the fool:
With mirth and laughter let old wrinkles come,
And let my liver rather heat with wine
Than my heart cool with mortifying groans.
Why should a man, whose blood is warm within,
Sit like his grandsire cut in alabaster?
Sleep when he wakes and creep into the jaundice
By being peevish? I tell thee what, Antonio—   90
I love thee, and it is my love that speaks—
There are a sort of men whose visages
Do cream and mantle like a standing pond,
And do a wilful stillness entertain,
With purpose to be dress'd in an opinion
Of wisdom, gravity, profound conceit,
As who should say 'I am Sir Oracle,
And when I ope my lips let no dog bark!'
O my Antonio, I do know of these
That therefore only are reputed wise   100
For saying nothing, when, I am very sure,
If they should speak, would almost damn those ears
Which, hearing them, would call their brothers fools.
I'll tell thee more of this another time;
But fish not, with this melancholy bait,
For this fool-gudgeon, this opinion.
Come, good Lorenzo.   Fare ye well awhile:
I'll end my exhortation after dinner.

Lorenzo.   Well, we will leave you then till dinner-time:
I must be one of these same dumb wise men,   110
For Gratiano never lets me speak.

Gratiano.   Well, keep me company but two years moe,
Thou shalt not know the sound of thine own tongue.

Antonio.   Farewell; I'll grow a talker for this gear.

Gra.   Thanks, i' faith, for silence is only commendable
In a neat's tongue dried.   [*Exeunt Gratiano and Lorenzo.*

Antonio.   Is that any thing now?

Bassanio.   Gratiano speaks an infinite deal of nothing,
more than any man in all Venice.   His reasons are as
two grains of wheat hid in two bushels of chaff: you
shall seek all day ere you find them, and when you have
them, they are not worth the search.   122

Antonio.   Well, tell me now what lady is the same
To whom you swore a secret pilgrimage,
That you to-day promised to tell me of?

Bassanio.   'Tis not unknown to you, Antonio,
How much I have disabled mine estate,
By something showing a more swelling port
Than my faint means would grant continuance:
Nor do I now make moan to be abridged   130
From such a noble rate; but my chief care
Is to come fairly off from the great debts
Wherein my time something too prodigal
Hath left me gaged.   To you, Antonio,
I owe the most, in money and in love,
And from your love I have a warranty
To unburden all my plots and purposes
How to get clear of all the debts I owe.

Antonio.   I pray you, good Bassanio, let me know it;
And if it stand, as you yourself still do,   140
Within the eye of honour, be assured,
My purse, my person, my extremest means,
Lie all unlock'd to your occasions.

Bassanio.   In my school-days, when I had lost one
          shaft
I shot his fellows of the self-same flight

The self-same way, with more advisèd watch,
To find the other forth, and by adventuring both
I oft found both: I urge this childhood proof,
Because what follows is pure innocence.   150
I owe you much, and, like a wilful youth,
That which I owe is lost; but if you please
To shoot another arrow that self way
Which you did shoot the first, I do not doubt,
As I will watch the aim, or to find both
Or bring your latter hazard back again
And thankfully rest debtor for the first.

    Antonio.   You know me well, and herein spend but
        time
To wind about my love with circumstance;   160
And out of doubt you do me now more wrong
In making question of my uttermost
Than if you had made waste of all I have:
Then do but say to me what I should do
That in you knowledge may by me be done,
And I am prest unto it: therefore, speak.

    Bassanio.   In Belmont is a lady richly left;
And she is fair and, fairer than that word,
Of wondrous virtues: sometimes from her eyes
I did receive fair speechless messages: 170
Her name is Portia, nothing undervalued
To Cato's daughter, Brutus' Portia:
Nor is the wide world ignorant of her worth,
For the four winds blow in from every coast
Renowned suitors, and her sunny locks
Hang on her temples like a golden fleece;
Which makes her seat of Belmont Colchos' strand,
And many Jasons came in quest of her.

O my Antonio, had I but the means
To hold a rival place with one of them,   180
I have a mind presages me such thrift,
That I should questionless be fortunate!

   Antonio.   Thou know'st that all my fortunes are at
      sea;
Neither have I money nor commodity
To raise a present sum: therefore go forth;
Try what my credit can in Venice do:
That shall be rack'd, even to the uttermost,
To furnish thee to Belmont, to fair Portia.
Go, presently inquire, and so will I,   190
Where money is, and I no question make
To have it of my trust or for my sake.   [*Exeunt*

    SCENE II.   *Belmont.   A room in Portia's house.*

        Enter PORTIA *and* NERISSA.

   Portia.   By my troth, Nerissa, my little body is aweary
of this great world.

   Nerissa.   You would be, sweet madam, if your miseries
were in the same abundance as your good fortunes are:
and yet, for aught I see, they are as sick that surfeit
with too much as they that starve with nothing.   It is
no mean happiness therefore, to be seated in the mean:
superfluity comes sooner by white hairs, but competency
lives longer.

   Portia.   Good sentences and well pronounced.   10

   Nerissa.   They would be better, if well followed.

   Portia.   If to do were as easy as to know what were
good to do, chapels had been churches and poor men's
cottages princes' palaces.   It is a good divine that follows
his own instructions: I can easier teach twenty what

were good to be done, than be one of the twenty to follow
mine own teaching. The brain may devise laws for the
blood, but a hot temper leaps o'er a cold decree: such a
hare is madness the youth, to skip o'er the meshes of
good counsel the cripple. But this reasoning is not in
the fashion to choose me a husband. O me, the word
'choose!' I may neither choose whom I would nor refuse
whom I dislike; so is the will of a living daughter curbed
by the will of a dead father. Is it not hard, Nerissa, that
I cannot choose one nor refuse none?   25

Nerissa. Your father was ever virtuous; and holy
men at their death have good inspirations: therefore the
lottery, that he hath devised in these three chests of gold,
silver and lead, whereof who chooses his meaning chooses
you, will, no doubt, never be chosen by any rightly but
one who shall rightly love. But what warmth is there
in your affection towards any of these princely suitors
that are already come?   33

Portia. I pray thee, over-name them; and as thou
namest them, I will describe them; and, according to my
description, level at my affection.

Nerissa. First, there is the Neapolitan prince.

Portia. Ay, that's a colt indeed, for he doth nothing
but talk of his horse; and he makes it a great appropriation to his own good parts, that he can shoe him himself.

Nerissa. Then there is the County Palatine.   41

Portia. He doth nothing but frown, as who should
say 'If you will not have me, choose:' he hears merry
tales and smiles not: I fear he will prove the weeping
philosopher when he grows old, being so full of unman-
nerly sadness in his youth. I had rather be married to

a death's head with a bone in his mouth than to either of these. God defend me from these two!

Nerissa. How say you by the French lord, Monsieur Le Bon?   50

Portia. God made him, and therefore let him pass for a man. In truth, I know it is a sin to be a mocker: but, he! why, he hath a horse better than the Neapolitan's, a better bad habit of frowning than the Count Palatine; he is every man in no man; if a throstle sing, he falls straight a capering: he will fence with his own shadow: if I should marry him, I should marry twenty husbands. If he would despise me, I would forgive him, for if he love me to madness, I shall never requite him.

Nerissa. What say you then to Falconbridge, the young baron of England?   61

Portia. You know I say nothing to him, for he understands not me, nor I him: he hath neither Latin, French, nor Italian, and you will come into the court and swear that I have a poor pennyworth in the English. He is a proper man's picture; but, alas, who can converse with a dumb-show? How oddly he is suited! I think he bought his doublet in Italy, his round hose in France, his bonnet in Germany and his behaviour every where.

Nerissa. What think you of the Scottish lord, his neighbour?   71

Portia. That he hath a neighbourly charity in him, for he borrowed a box of the ear of the Englishman and swore he would pay him again when he was able: I think the Frenchman became his surety and sealed under for another.

Nerissa. How like you the young German, the Duke of Saxony's nephew?

Portia. Very vilely in the morning, when he is sober, and most vilely in the afternoon, when he is drunk: when he is best, he is a little worse than a man, and when he is worst, he is little better than a beast: an the worst fall that ever fell, I hope I shall make shift to go without him.   84

Nerissa. If he should offer to choose, and choose the right casket, you should refuse to perform your father's will, if you should refuse to accept him.

Portia. Therefore, for fear of the worst, I pray thee, set a deep glass of Rhenish wine on the contrary casket, for if the devil be within and that temptation without, I know he will choose it. I will do any thing, Nerissa, ere I'll be married to a sponge   92

Nerissa. You need not fear, lady, the having any of these lords; they have acquainted me with their determinations; which is, indeed, to return to their home and to trouble you with no more suit, unless you may be won by some other sort than your father's imposition depending on the caskets.

Portia. If I live to be as old as Sibylla, I will die as chaste as Diana, unless I be obtained by the manner of my father's will. I am glad this parcel of wooers are so reasonable, for there is not one among them but I dote on his very absence, and I pray God grant them a fair departure.   104

Nerissa. Do you not remember, lady, in your father's time, a Venetian, a scholar and a soldier, that came hither in company of the Marquis of Montferrat?

Portia.   Yes, yes, it was Bassanio; as I think, he was so called.

Nerissa.   True, madam: he, of all the men that ever my foolish eyes looked upon, was the best deserving a fair lady.

Portia.   I remember him well, and I remember him worthy of thy praise.   114

Enter a Serving-man.

How now! what news?

Serv.   The four strangers seek for you, madam, to take their leave: and there is a forerunner come from a fifth, the Prince of Morocco, who brings word the prince his master will be here to-night

Portia.   If I could bid the fifth welcome with so good a heart as I can bid the other four farewell, I should be glad of his approach: if he have the condition of a saint and the complexion of a devil, I had rather he should shrive me than wive me.   124

Come, Nerissa.   Sirrah, go before.

Whiles we shut the gates upon one wooer, another knocks
     at the door.   [*Exeunt.*

Scene III.   *Venice.   A public place.*

Enter BASSANIO *and* SHYLOCK.

Shylock.   Three thousand ducats; well.

Bassanio.   Ay, sir, for three months.

Shylock.   For three months; well.

Bassanio.   For the which, as I told you, Antonio shall be bound.

Shylock.   Antonio shall become bound; well.

Bassanio. May you stead me? will you pleasure me? shall I know your answer?

Shylock. Three thousand ducats, for three months, and Antonio bound.   10

Bassanio. Your answer to that.

Shylock. Antonio is a good man.

Bass. Have you heard any imputation to the contrary?

Shylock. Oh, no no, no, no: my meaning in saying he is a good man is to have you understand me that he is sufficient. Yet his means are in supposition: he hath an argosy bound to Tripolis, another to the Indies; I understand, moreover, upon the Rialto, he hath a third at Mexico, a fourth for England, and other ventures he hath, squandered abroad. But ships are but boards, sailors but men: there be land-rats and water-rats, water-thieves and land-thieves, I mean pirates, and then there is the peril of waters, winds and rocks. The man is, notwithstanding, sufficient. Three thousand ducats; I think I may take his bond.

Bassanio. Be assured you may.

Shylock. I will be assured I may; and, that I may be assured, I will bethink me. May I speak with Antonio?

Bassanio. If it please you to dine with us.   30

Shylock. Yes, to smell pork; to eat of the habitation which your prophet the Nazarite conjured the devil into. I will buy with you, sell with you, talk with you, walk with you, and so following, but I will not eat with you, drink with you, nor pray with you. What news on the Rialto? Who is he comes here?

Enter ANTONIO.

Bassanio.   This is Signior Antonio.

Shylock. [*Aside*] How like a fawning publican he looks!
I hate him for he is a Christian,
But more for that in low simplicity   40
He lends out money gratis and brings down
The rate of usance here with us in Venice.
If I can catch him once upon the hip,
I will feed fat the ancient grudge I bear him.
He hates our sacred nation, and he rails,
Even there where merchants most do congregate,
On me, my bargains and my well-won thrift,
Which he calls interest.   Cursèd be my tribe,
If I forgive him!

Bassanio.   Shylock, do you hear?   50

Shylock.   I am debating of my present store,
And, by the near guess of my memory,
I cannot instantly raise up the gross
Of full three thousand ducats.   What of that?
Tubal, a wealthy Hebrew of my tribe,
Will furnish me.   But soft! how many months
Do you desire? [*To Ant.*]   Rest you fair, good signior;
Your worship was the last man in our mouths.

Antonio.   Shylock, although I neither lend nor borrow
By taking nor by giving of excess,   60
Yet, to supply the ripe wants of my friend,
I'll break a custom. [*To Bassanio.*] Is he yet possess'd
How much ye would?

Shylock.   Ay, ay, three thousand ducats.

Antonio.   And for three months.

Shylock. I had forgot; three months; you told me so.
Well then, your bond; and let me see; but hear you;
Methought you said you neither lend nor borrow
Upon advantage.

Antonio.   I do never use it.   70

Shylock. When Jacob grazed his uncle Laban's sheep—
This Jacob from our holy Abram was,
As his wise mother wrought in his behalf,
The third possessor; ay, he was the third—

Antonio. And what of him? did he take interest?

Shylock. No, not take interest, not, as you would say,
Directly interest: mark what Jacob did
When Laban and himself were compromised
That all the eanlings which were streak'd and pied
Should fall as Jacob's hire.   80
This was a way to thrive, and he was blest;
And thrift is blessing, if men steal it not.

Antonio. This was a venture, sir, that Jacob served for;
A thing not in his power to bring to pass,
But sway'd and fashion'd by the hand of heaven.
Was this inserted to make interest good?
Or is your gold and silver ewes and rams?

Shylock. I cannot tell; I make it breed as fast:
But note me, signior.

Antonio.   Mark you this, Bassanio,   90
The devil can cite Scripture for his purpose.
An evil soul producing holy witness
Is like a villain with a smiling cheek,
A goodly apple rotten at the heart:
O, what a goodly outside falsehood hath!

Shylock. Three thousand ducats; 'tis a good round sum.
Three months from twelve; then, let me see; the rate—

Antonio.   Well, Shylock, shall we be beholding to you?

Shylock.   Signior Antonio, many a time and oft
In the Rialto you have rated me   100
About my moneys and my usances:
Still have I borne it with a patient shrug,
For sufferance is the badge of all our tribe.
You call me misbeliever, cut-throat dog,
And spit upon my Jewish gaberdine,
And all for use of that which is mine own.
Well then, it now appears you need my help:
Go to, then; you come to me, and you say
'Shylock, we would have moneys:' you say so;
You, that did void your rheum upon my beard   110
And foot me as you spurn a stranger cur
Over your threshold: moneys is your suit.
What should I say to you?   Should I not say
'Hath a dog money? is it possible
A cur can lend three thousand ducats?'   Or
Shall I bend low and in a bondman's key,
With bated breath and whispering humbleness,
Say this;
'Fair sir, you spit on me on Wednesday last;
You spurn'd me such a day; another time   120
You call'd me dog; and for these courtesies
I'll lend you thus much moneys?'

Antonio.   I am as like to call thee so again,
To spit on thee again, to spurn thee too.
If thou wilt lend this money, lend it not
As to thy friends; for when did friendship take
A breed for barren metal of his friend?
But lend it rather to thine enemy,

Who if he break, thou mayst with better face
Exact the penalty.   130

   Shylock.   Why, look you, how you storm!
I would be friends with you and have your love,
Forget the shames that you have stain'd me with,
Supply your present wants and take no doit
Of usance for my moneys, and you'll not hear me:
This is kind I offer.

   Bassanio.   This were kindness.

   Shylock.   This kindness will I show.
Go with me to a notary, seal me there
Your single bond; and, in a merry sport,   140
If you repay me not on such a day,
In such a place, such sum or sums as are
Express'd in the condition, let the forfeit
Be nominated for an equal pound
Of your fair flesh, to be cut off and taken
In what part of your body pleaseth me.

   Antonio.   Content, i' faith: I'll seal to such a bond
And say there is much kindness in the Jew.

   Bassanio.   You shall not seal to such a bond for me:
I'll rather dwell in my necessity.   150

   Antonio: Why, fear not, man; I will not forfeit it:
Within these two months, that's a month before
This bond expires, I do expect return
Of thrice three times the value of this bond.

   Shylock.   O father Abram, what these Christians are,
Whose own hard dealings teaches them suspect
The thoughts of others!   Pray you, tell me this;
If he should break his day, what should I gain
By the exaction of the forfeiture?

A pound of man's flesh taken from a man   160
Is not so estimable, profitable neither,
As flesh of muttons, beefs, or goats.   I say,
To buy his favour, I extend this friendship:
If he will take it, so; if not, adieu;
And, for my love, I pray you wrong me not.

Antonio.   Yes, Shylock, I will seal unto this bond.

Shylock.   Then meet me forthwith at the notary's;
Give him direction for this merry bond,
And I will go and purse the ducats straight,
See to my house, left in the fearful guard   170
Of an unthrifty knave, and presently
I will be with you.

Antonio.   Hie thee, gentle Jew.   [*Exit Shylock.*
The Hebrew will turn Christian: he grows kind.

Bassanio.   I like not fair terms and a villain's mind.

Antonio.   Come on: in this there can be no dismay;
My ships come home a month before the day.   [*Exeunt.*

ACT II.

Scene I.   *Belmont.   A room in Portia's house.*

Flourish of Cornets.   Enter the Prince of Morocco *and his train,*
Portia, Nerissa, *and others attending.*

Morocco.   Mislike me not for my complexion,
The shadow'd livery of the burnish'd sun,
To whom I am a neighbour and near bred.
Bring me the fairest creature northward born,
Where Phœbus' fire scarce thaws the icicles,
And let us make incision for your love,
To prove whose blood is reddest, his or mine.
I tell thee, lady, this aspect of mine

Hath fear'd the valiant: by my love, I swear
The best-regarded virgins of our clime   10
Have loved it too: I would not change this hue,
Except to steal your thoughts, my gentle queen.

   Portia.   In terms of choice I am not solely led
By nice direction of a maiden's eyes;
Besides, the lottery of my destiny
Bars me the right of voluntary choosing;
But if my father had not scanted me,
And hedged me by his wit, to yield myself
His wife who wins me by that means I told you,
Yourself, renowned prince, then stood as fair   20
As any comer I have look'd on yet
For my affection.

   Morocco.   Even for that I thank you:
Therefore, I pray you, lead me to the caskets
To try my fortune.   By this scimitar,
That slew the Sophy and a Persian prince
That won three fields of Sultan Solyman,
I would outstare the sternest eyes that look,
Outbrave the heart most daring on the earth,
Pluck, the young sucking cubs from the she-bear,   30
Yea, mock the lion when he roars for prey,
To win thee, lady.   But, alas the while!
If Hercules and Lichas play at dice
Which is the better man, the greater throw
May turn by fortune from the weaker hand:
So is Alcides beaten by his page;
And so may I, blind fortune leading me,
Miss that which one unworthier may attain,
And die with grieving.

Portia.   You must take your chance,   40
And either not attempt to choose at all
Or swear, before you choose, if you choose wrong
Never to speak to lady afterward
In way of marriage: therefore be advised.

Morocco.   Nor will not.   Come, bring me unto my
        chance.

Portia.   First, forward to the temple: after dinner
Your hazard shall be made.

Morocco.   Good fortune then!
To make me blest or cursed'st among men.   50

                            [*Cornets, and exeunt.*

          SCENE II.   *Venice.   A street.*

              Enter LAUNCELOT.

Launcelot.   Certainly my conscience will serve me to
run from this Jew my master.   The fiend is at mine elbow
and tempts me, saying to me 'Gobbo, Launcelot Gobbo,
good Launcelot,' or 'good Gobbo,' or 'good Launcelot
Gobbo, use your legs, take the start, run away.'   My
conscience says 'No; take heed, honest Launcelot; take
heed, honest Gobbo,' or, as aforesaid, 'honest Launcelot
Gobbo; do not run; scorn running with thy heels.'
Well, the most courageous fiend bids me pack: 'Via!'
says the fiend; 'away!' says the fiend; 'for the heavens,
rouse up a brave mind,' says the fiend, 'and run.'   Well,
my conscience, hanging about the neck of my heart, says
very wisely to me 'My honest friend Launcelot, being an
honest man's son,' or rather an honest woman's son; for
indeed my father did something smack, something grow
to, he had a kind of taste; well, my conscience says

'Launcelot, budge not.' 'Budge,' says the fiend. 'Budge not,' says my conscience. 'Conscience,' says I, 'you counsel well;' 'Fiend,' say I, 'you counsel well:' to be ruled by my conscience, I should stay with the Jew my master, who, God bless the mark, is a kind of devil; and, to run away from the Jew, I should be ruled by the fiend, who, saving your reverence, is the devil himself. Certainly the Jew is the very devil incarnal; and, in my conscience, my conscience is but a kind of hard conscience, to offer to counsel me to stay with the Jew. The fiend gives the more friendly counsel: I will run, fiend; my heels are at your command; I will run.

Enter Old GOBBO, *with a basket.*

Gobbo. Master young man, you, I pray you, which is the way to master Jew's?   30

Launcelot. [*Aside*] O heavens, this is my true-begotten father! who, being more than sand-blind, high-gravel-blind, knows me not: I will try confusions with him.

Gobbo. Master young gentleman, I pray you, which is the way to master Jew's?

Launcelot. Turn up on your right hand at the next turning, but, at the next turning of all, on your left, marry, at the very next turning, turn of no hand, but turn down indirectly to the Jew's house.

Gobbo. By God's sonties, 'twill be a hard way to hit. Can you tell me whether one Launcelot, that dwells with him, dwell with him or no?   42

Launcelot. Talk you of young Master Launcelot? [*Aside*] Mark me now; now will I raise the waters.—Talk you of young Master Launcelot?

Gobbo. No master, sir, but a poor man's son: his father, though I say it, is an honest exceeding poor man and, God be thanked, well to live.

Launcelot. Well, let his father be what a' will, we talk of young Master Launcelot.   50

Gobbo. Your worship's friend and Launcelot, sir.

Launcelot. But I pray you, ergo, old man, ergo, I beseech you, talk you of young Master Launcelot?

Gobbo. Of Launcelot, an't please your mastership.

Launcelot. Ergo, Master Launcelot. Talk not of Master Launcelot, father; for the young gentleman, according to Fate and Destinies and such odd sayings, the Sisters Three and such branches of learning, is indeed deceased, or, as you would say in plain terms, gone to heaven.   60

Gobbo. Marry, God forbid! the boy was the very staff of my age, my very prop.

Launcelot. Do I look like a cudgel or a hovel-post, a staff or a prop? Do you know me, father?

Gobbo. Alack the day, I know you not, young gentleman: but, I pray you, tell me, is my boy, God rest his soul, alive or dead?

Launcelot. Do you not know me, father?

Gobbo. Alack, sir, I am sand-blind; I know you not.

Launcelot. Nay, indeed, if you had your eyes, you might fail of the knowing me: it is a wise father that knows his own child. Well, old man, I will tell you news of your son: give me your blessing: truth will come to light; murder cannot be hid long; a man's son may, but at the length truth will out.

Gobbo.   Pray you, sir, stand up; I am sure you are not Launcelot, my boy.

Launcelot.   Pray you, let's have no more fooling about it, but give me your blessing: I am Launcelot, your boy that was, your son that is, your child that shall be.   80

Gobbo.   I cannot think you are my son.

Launcelot.   I know not what I shall think of that, but I am Launcelot, the Jew's man, and I am sure Margery your wife is my mother.

Gobbo.   Her name is Margery, indeed: I'll be sworn, if thou be Launcelot, thou art mine own flesh and blood. Lord worshipped might he be! what a beard hast thou got! thou hast got more hair on thy chin than Dobbin my fill-horse has on his tail.

Launcelot.   It should seem then that Dobbin's tail grows backward: I am sure he had more hair of his tail than I have of my face when I last saw him.   92

Gobbo.   Lord, how art thou changed! How dost thou and thy master agree? I have brought him a present. How 'gree you now!

Launcelot.   Well, well: but, for mine own part, as I have set up my rest to run away, so I will not rest till I have run some ground. My master's a very Jew: give him a present! give him a halter: I am famished in his service; you may tell every finger I have with my ribs. Father, I am glad you are come: give me your present to one Master Bassanio, who indeed gives rare new liveries: if I serve not him, I will run as far as God has any ground. O rare fortune! here comes the man: to him, father; for I am a Jew, if I serve the Jew any longer.

Enter BASSANIO, *with* LEONARDO *and other followers.*

Bassanio.   You may do so; but let it be so hasted
that supper be ready at the farthest by five of the clock.
See these letters delivered; put the liveries to making,
and desire Gratiano to come anon to my lodging.   110

[*Exit a Servant.*

Launcelot.   To him, father.

Gobbo.   God bless your worship!

Bassanio.   Gramercy! wouldst thou aught with me?

Gobbo.   Here's my son, sir, a poor boy,—

Launcelot.   Not a poor boy, sir, but the rich Jew's
man; that would, sir, as my father shall specify—

Gobbo.   He hath a great infection, sir, as one would
say, to serve—

Launcelot.   Indeed, the short and the long is, I serve
the Jew, and have a desire, as my father shall specify,—

Gobbo.   His master and he, saving your worship's
reverence, are scarce cater-cousins—   122

Launcelot.   To be brief, the very truth is that the Jew,
having done me wrong, doth cause me, as my father,
being, I hope, an old man, shall frutify unto you,—

Gobbo.   I have here a dish of doves that I would
bestow upon your worship, and my suit is—

Launcelot.   In very brief, the suit is impertinent to
myself, as your worship shall know by this honest old
man; and, though I say it, though old man, yet poor man,
my father.

Bassanio.   One speak for both. What would you?   132

Launcelot.   Serve you, sir.

Gobbo.   That is the very defect of the matter, sir.

Bassanio.   I know thee well; thou hast obtain'd thy
suit:
Shylock thy master spoke with me this day,
And hath preferr'd thee, if it be preferment
To leave a rich Jew's service, to become
The follower of so poor a gentleman.   140

Launcelot.   The old proverb is very well parted
between my master Shylock and you, sir: you have the
grace of God, sir, and he hath enough.

Bass.   Thou speak'st it well. Go, father, with thy son.
Take leave of thy old master and inquire
My lodging out.   Give him a livery
More guarded than his fellows': see it done.

Launcelot.   Father, in.   I cannot get a service, no; I
have ne'er a tongue in my head.   Well, if any man in
Italy have a fairer table which doth offer to swear upon
a book, I shall have good fortune.   Go to, here's a simple
line of life: here's a small trifle of wives: alas, fifteen
wives is nothing! eleven widows and nine maids is a
simple coming-in for one man: and then to 'scape
drowning thrice, and to be in peril of my life with the
edge of a feather-bed; here are simple 'scapes.   Well, if
Fortune be a woman, she's a good wench for this gear.
Father, come; I'll take my leave of the Jew in the
twinkling of an eye.   159

[*Exeunt Launcelot and Old Gobbo.*

Bassanio.   I pray thee, good Leonardo, think on this:
These things being bought and orderly bestow'd
Return in haste, for I do feast to-night
My best-esteem'd acquaintance; hie thee, go.

Leonardo.   My best endeavours shall be done herein.

Enter GRATIANO.

Gratiano. Where is your master?

Leonardo. Yonder, sir, he walks. [*Exit.*

Gratiano Signior Bassanio!

Bassanio. Gratiano!

Gratiano. I have a suit to you.

Bassanio. You have obtain'd it. 170

Gratiano. You must not deny me: I must go with
you to Belmont.

Bass. Why then you must. But hear thee, Gratiano;
Thou art too wild, too rude and bold of voice;
Parts that become thee happily enough
And in such eyes as ours appear not faults;
But where thou art not known, why, there they show
Something too liberal. Pray thee, take pain
To allay with some cold drops of modesty
Thy skipping spirit, lest through thy wild behaviour 180
I be misconstrued in the place I go to
And lose my hopes.

Gratiano. Signior Bassanio, hear me:
If I do not put on a sober habit,
Talk with respect and swear but now and then,
Wear prayer-books in my pocket, look demurely,
Nay more, while grace is saying, hood mine eyes
Thus with my hat, and sigh and say 'amen,'
Use all the observance of civility,
Like one well studied in a sad ostent 190
To please his grandam, never trust me more.

Bassanio. Well, we shall see your bearing.

Gra. Nay, but I bar to-night: you shall not gauge me
By what we do to-night.

Bassanio.   No, that were pity:
I would entreat you rather to put on
Your boldest suit of mirth, for we have friends
That purpose merriment.   But fare you well:
I have some business.

Gratiano.   And I must to Lorenzo and the rest: 200
But we will visit you at supper-time.   [*Exeunt.*

SCENE III.   *The same.   A room in Shylock's house.*

Enter JESSICA *and* LAUNCELOT.

Jessica.   I am sorry thou wilt leave my father so:
Our house is hell, and thou, a merry devil,
Didst rob it of some taste of tediousness.
But fare thee well, there is a ducat for thee:
And, Launcelot, soon at supper shalt thou see
Lorenzo, who is thy new master's guest:
Give him this letter; do it secretly;
And so farewell: I would not have my father
See me in talk with thee.   9

Launcelot.   Adieu! tears exhibit my tongue.   Most
beautiful pagan, most sweet Jew, adieu: these foolish
drops do something drown my manly spirit: adieu.

Jessica.   Farewell, good Launcelot.   [*Exit Launcelot.*
Alack, what heinous sin is it in me
To be ashamed to be my father's child!
But though I am a daughter to his blood,
I am not to his manners.   O Lorenzo,
If thou keep promise, I shall end this strife,
Become a Christian and thy loving wife.   [*Exit.*

SCENE IV. *The same. A street*

Enter GRATIANO, LORENZO, SALARINO, *and* SALANIO.

Lorenzo.   Nay, we will slink away in supper-time,
Disguise us at my lodging and return
All in an hour.

Gratiano.   We have not made good preparation.

Salarino.   We have not spoke us yet of torch-bearers.

Salanio.   'Tis vile, unless it may be quaintly order'd,
And better in my mind not undertook.

Lorenzo.   'Tis now but four o'clock: we have two
  hours
To furnish us.   10

Enter LAUNCELOT, *with a letter.*

Friend Launcelot, what's the news?

Launcelot.   An it shall please you to break up this, it
shall seem to signify.

Lorenzo.   I know the hand: in faith, 'tis a fair hand,
And whiter than the paper it writ on
Is the fair hand that writ.

Gratiano.   Love-news, in faith.

Launcelot.   By your leave, sir.

Lorenzo.   Whither goest thou?

Launcelot.   Marry sir, to bid my old master the Jew
to sup to-night with my new master the Christian.   21

Lorenzo.   Hold here, take this: tell gentle Jessica
I will not fail her; speak it privately.   [*Exit Launcelot.*
Go, gentlemen,
Will you prepare you for this masque to-night?
I am provided of a torch-bearer.

Salarino.   Ay, marry, I'll be gone about it straight.

Salanio.   And so will I.

Lorenzo   Meet me and Gratiano
At Gratiano's lodging some hour hence.   30

Salarino.   'Tis good we do so. [*Exeunt Salarino and Salanio*

Gratiano.   Was not that letter from fair Jessica?

Lorenzo.   I must needs tell thee all. She hath directed
How I shall take her from her father's house,
What gold and jewels she is furnish'd with,
What page's suit she hath in readiness.
If e'er the Jew her father come to heaven,
It will be for his gentle daughter's sake:
And never dare misfortune cross her foot,
Unless she do it under this excuse,   40
That she is issue to a faithless Jew.
Come, go with me; peruse this as thou goest:
Fair Jessica shall be my torch-bearer.   [*Exeunt.*

SCENE V.   *The same.   Before Shylock's house.*

Enter SHYLOCK *and* LAUNCELOT.

Shylock.   Well, thou shalt see, thy eyes shall be thy
        judge,
The difference of old Shylock and Bassanio:—
What, Jessica!—thou shalt not gormandize,
As thou hast done with me:—What, Jessica!—
And sleep and snore, and rend apparel out:—
Why, Jessica, I say!

Launcelot.   Why, Jessica!

Shylock.   Who bids thee call?   I do not bid thee call.

Launcelot.   Your worship was wont to tell me that I
could do nothing without bidding.   11

Enter JESSICA.

Jessica.   Call you? what is your will?

Shylock.   I am bid forth to supper, Jessica:
There are my keys.   But wherefore should I go?
I am not bid for love; they flatter me:
But yet I'll go in hate, to feed upon
The prodigal Christian.   Jessica, my girl,
Look to my house.   I am right loath to go:
There is some ill a-brewing towards my rest,
For I did dream of money-bags to-night.   20

Launcelot.   I beseech you, sir, go: my young master
doth expect your reproach.

Shylock.   So do I his.

Launcelot.   An they have conspired together, I will
not say you shall see a masque; but if you do, then it
was not for nothing that my nose fell a-bleeding on
Black-Monday last at six o'clock i' the morning, falling
out that year on Ash-Wednesday was four year, in the
afternoon.

Shy.   What, are there masques? Hear you me, Jessica:
Lock up my doors; and when you hear the drum
And the vile squealing of the wry-neck'd fife,   32
Clamber not you up to the casements then,
Nor thrust your head into the public street
To gaze on Christian fools with varnish'd faces,
But stop my house's ears, I mean my casements:
Let not the sound of shallow foppery enter
My sober house.   By Jacob's staff I swear,
I have no mind of feasting forth to-night:
But I will go.   Go you before me, sirrah;   40
Say I will come.

Launcelot.   I will go before, sir.   Mistress, look out
at window, for all this;

> There will come a Christian by,
> Will be worth a Jewess' eye.   [*Exit.*

Shylock.   What says that fool of Hagar's offspring, ha?

Jess.   His words were 'Farewell mistress;' nothing else.

Shylock.   The patch is kind enough, but a huge feeder;
Snail-slow in profit, and he sleeps by day
More than the wild-cat; drones hive not with me: 50
Therefore I part with him, and part with him
To one that I would have him help to waste
His borrow'd purse.   Well, Jessica, go in:
Perhaps I will return immediately:
Do as I bid you; shut doors after you:
Fast bind, fast find;
A proverb never stale in thrifty mind.   [*Exit.*

Jessica.   Farewell; and if my fortune be not crost,
I have a father, you a daughter, lost.   [*Exit.*

Scene VI. *The same.*

Enter Gratiano *and* Salarino, *masqued.*

Gratiano.   This is the pent-house under which Lorenzo
Desired us to make stand.

Salarino.   His hour is almost past.

Gratiano.   And it is marvel he out-dwells his hour,
For lovers ever run before the clock

Salarino.   O, ten times faster Venus' pigeons fly
To seal love's bonds new-made, than they are wont
To keep obliged faith unforfeited

Gratiano.   That ever holds: who riseth from a feast
With that keen appetite that he sits down?   10

Where is the horse that doth untread again
His tedious measures with the unbated fire
That he did pace them first? All things that are
Are with more spirit chased than enjoy'd.
How like a younker or a prodigal
The scarfed bark puts from her native bay,
Hugg'd and embraced by the wanton wind!
How like the prodigal doth she return,
With over-weather'd ribs and ragged sails,
Lean, rent and beggar'd by the wanton wind!   20

Salarino.   Here comes Lorenzo: more of this hereafter.

Enter LORENZO.

Lorenzo.   Sweet friends, your patience for my long
      abode;
Not I, but my affairs, have made you wait:
When you shall please to play the thieves for wives,
I'll watch as long for you then.   Approach;
Here dwells my father Jew.   Ho! who's within?

Enter JESSICA, *above, in boy's clothes.*

Jessica.   Who are you? Tell me, for more certainty,
Albeit I'll swear that I do know your tongue.

Lorenzo.   Lorenzo, and thy love   30

Jessica.   Lorenzo, certain, and my love indeed,
For who love I so much?   And now who knows
But you, Lorenzo, whether I am yours?

Lorenzo.   Heaven and thy thoughts are witness that
      thou art.

Jessica.   Here, catch this casket; it is worth the pains.
I am glad 'tis night, you do not look on me,
For I am much ashamed of my exchange:

But love is blind and lovers cannot see
The pretty follies that themselves commit;   40
For if they could, Cupid himself would blush
To see me thus transformed to a boy.

Lorenzo.   Descend, for you must be my torch-bearer.

Jessica.   What, must I hold a candle to my shames?
They in themselves, good sooth, are too too light.
Why, 'tis an office of discovery, love;
And I should be obscured.

Lorenzo.   So are you, sweet,
Even in the lovely garnish of a boy.
But come at once;   50
For the close night doth play the runaway,
And we are stay'd for at Bassanio's feast.

Jessica.   I will make fast the doors, and gild myself
With some more ducats, and be with you straight.

                    [*Exit above.*

Gratiano.   Now, by my hood, a Gentile and no Jew.

Lorenzo.   Beshrew me but I love her heartily;
For she is wise, if I can judge of her,
And fair she is, if that mine eyes be true,
And true she is, as she hath proved herself,
And therefore, like herself, wise, fair and true,   60
Shall she be placed in my constant soul.

                    Enter JESSICA *below.*

What, art thou come?   On, gentleman; away!
Our masquing mates by this time for us stay.

                    [*Exit with Jessica and Salarino.*

                    Enter ANTONIO.

Antonio.   Who's there?

Gratiano.   Signior Antonio!

Antonio. Fie, fie, Gratiano! where are all the rest?
'Tis nine o'clock: our friends all stay for you.
No masque to-night; the wind is come about;
Bassanio presently will go aboard:
I have sent twenty out to seek for you.   70

Gratiano. I am glad on't: I desire no more delight
Than to be under sail and gone to-night.   [*Exeunt.*

SCENE VII. *Belmont. A room in Portia's house.*

Flourish of Cornets. Enter the PRINCE OF ARRAGON, PORTIA, *and
their trains.*

Portia. Go draw aside the curtains and discover
The several caskets to this noble prince.
Now make your choice.

Morocco. The first, of gold, who this inscription bears,
'Who chooseth me shall gain what many men desire;'
The second, silver, which this promise carries,
'Who chooseth me shall get as much as he deserves;'
This third, dull lead, with warning all as blunt,
'Who chooseth me must give and hazard all he hath.'
How shall I know if I do choose the right?   10

Portia. The one of them contains my picture, prince:
If you choose that, then I am yours withal.

Morocco. Some god direct my judgment! Let me see;
I will survey the inscriptions back again.
What says this leaden casket?
'Who chooseth me must give and hazard all he hath.'
Must give! for what? for lead! hazard for lead?
This casket threatens. Men that hazard all
Do it in hope of fair advantages:
A golden mind stoops not to shows of dross;   20

I'll then nor give nor hazard aught for lead.
What says the silver with her virgin hue?
'Who chooseth me shall get as much as he deserves.'
As much as he deserves! Pause there, Morocco,
And weigh thy value with an even hand:
If thou be'st rated by thy estimation,
Thou dost deserve enough; and yet enough
May not extend so far as to the lady:
And yet to be afeard of my deserving
Were but a weak disabling of myself.   30
As much as I deserve!   Why, that's the lady:
I do in birth deserve her, and in fortunes,
In graces and in qualities of breeding;
But more than these, in love I do deserve.
What if I stray'd no further, but chose here?
Let's see once more this saying graved in gold;
'Who chooseth me shall gain what many men desire.'
Why, that's the lady; all the world desires her;
From the four corners of the earth they come,
To kiss this shrine, this mortal breathing saint: 40
The Hyrcanian deserts and the vasty wilds
Of wide Arabia are as throughfares now
For princes to come view fair Portia:
The watery kingdom, whose ambitious head
Spits in the face of heaven, is no bar
To stop the foreign spirits, but they come,
As o'er a brook, to see fair Portia.
One of these three contains her heavenly picture.
Is't like that lead contains her?   'Twere damnation
To think so base a thought: it were too gross   50
To rib her cerecloth in the obscure grave.
Or shall I think in silver she's immured,

Being ten times undervalued to tried gold?
O sinful thought!   Never so rich a gem
Was set in worse than gold.   They have in England
A coin that bears the figure of an angel
Stamped in gold, but that's insculp'd upon;
But here an angel in a golden bed
Lies all within.   Deliver me the key:
Here do I choose, and thrive I as I may!   60

   Portia.   There, take it, prince; and if my form lie
        there,
Then I am yours.   [*He unlocks the golden casket.*

   Morocco.   O hell! what have we here?
A carrion Death, within whose empty eye
There is a written scroll: I'll read the writing.

   [*Reads*] "All that glisters is not gold;
            Often have you heard that told:
            Many a man his life hath sold
            But my outside to behold: 70
            Gilded tombs do worms infold.
            Had you been as wise as bold,
            Young in limbs, in judgment old,
            Your answer had not been inscroll'd:
            Fare you well; your suit is cold."

      Cold, indeed; and labour lost:
         Then, farewell, heat, and welcome, frost!
Portia, adieu.   I have too grieved a heart
To take a tedious leave: thus losers part.

                 [*Exit with his train. Flourish of Cornets.*

   Portia.   A gentle riddance.   Draw the curtains, go. 80
Let all of his complexion choose me so.   [*Exeunt.*

SCENE VIII. *Venice. A street.*

Enter SALARINO *and* SALANIO.

Salarino. Why, man, I saw Bassanio under sail:
With him is Gratiano gone along;
And in their ship I am sure Lorenzo is not.

Salanio. The villain Jew with outcries raised the
      duke,
Who went with him to search Bassanio's ship.

Salarino. He came too late, the ship was under sail:
But there the duke was given to understand
That in a gondola were seen together
Lorenzo and his amorous Jessica: 10
Besides, Antonio certified the duke
They were not with Bassanio in his ship.

Salanio. I never heard a passion so confused,
So strange, outrageous, and so variable,
As the dog Jew did utter in the streets:
'My daughter! O my ducats! O my daughter!
Fled with a Christian! O my Christian ducats!
Justice! the law! my ducats, and my daughter!
A sealed bag, two sealed bags of ducats,
Of double ducats, stolen from me by my daughter! 20
And jewels, two stones, two rich and precious stones,
Stolen by my daughter! Justice! find the girl;
She hath the stones upon her, and the ducats.'

Salarino. Why, all the boys in Venice follow him.
Crying, his stones, his daughter, and his ducats.

Salanio. Let good Antonio look he keep his day,
Or he shall pay for this.

Salarino.   Marry, well remember'd.
I reason'd with a Frenchman yesterday,

Who told me, in the narrow seas that part   30
The French and English, there miscarried
A vessel of our country richly fraught:
I thought upon Antonio when he told me,
And wish'd in silence that it were not his.

Salanio.   You were best to tell Antonio what you hear;
Yet do not suddenly, for it may grieve him.

Salarino.   A kinder gentleman treads not the earth,
I saw Bassanio and Antonio part:
Bassanio told him he would make some speed
Of his return: he answer'd, 'Do not so;   40
Slubber not business for my sake, Bassanio,
But stay the very riping of the time;
And for the Jew's bond which he hath of me,
Let it not enter in your mind of love:
Be merry, and employ your chiefest thoughts
To courtship and such fair ostents of love
As shall conveniently become you there:'
And even there, his eye being big with tears,
Turning his face, he put his hand behind him,
And with affection wondrous sensible   50
He wrung Bassanio's hand; and so they parted.

Salanio.   I think he only loves the world for him.
I pray thee, let us go and find him out
And quicken his embraced heaviness
With some delight or other.

Salarino   Do we so.   [*Exeunt.*

SCENE IX. *Belmont. A room in Portia's house.*

Enter NERISSA *with a* Servitor.

Ner. Quick, quick, I pray thee; draw the curtain
    straight:
The Prince of Arragon hath ta'en his oath,
And comes to his election presently.

Flourish of Cornets. Enter the PRINCE OF ARRAGON, PORTIA, *and
their trains.*

Portia. Behold, there stand the caskets, noble prince;
If you choose that wherein I am contain'd,
Straight shall our nuptial rites be solemnized;
But if you fail, without more speech, my lord,
You must be gone from hence immediately.

Arragon. I am enjoin'd by oath to observe three
    things: 11
First, never to unfold to any one
Which casket 'twas I chose; next, if I fail
Of the right casket, never in my life
To woo a maid in way of marriage:
Lastly,
If I do fail in fortune of my choice,
Immediately to leave you and be gone.

Portia. To these injunctions every one doth swear
That comes to hazard for my worthless self.   20

Arragon. And so have I address'd me. Fortune now
To my heart's hope!   Gold; silver; and base lead.
'Who chooseth me must give and hazard all he hath.'
You shall look fairer, ere I give or hazard.
What says the golden chest? ha! let me see:
'Who chooseth me shall gain what many men desire.'

What many men desire! that 'many' may be meant
By the fool multitude, that choose by show,
Not learning more than the fond eye doth teach;
Which pries not to the interior, but, like the martlet,   30
Builds in the weather on the outward wall,
Even in the force and road of casualty.
I will not choose what many men desire,
Because I will not jump with common spirits
And rank me with the barbarous multitudes.
Why, then to thee, thou silver treasure-house;
Tell me once more what title thou dost bear:
'Who chooseth me shall get as much as he deserves:'
And well said too; for who shall go about
To cozen fortune and be honourable   40
Without the stamp of merit?   Let none presume
To wear an undeserved dignity:
O, that estates, degrees and offices
Were not derived corruptly, and that clear honour
Were purchased by the merit of the wearer!
How many then should cover that stand bare!
How many be commanded that command!
How much low peasantry would then be glean'd
From the true seed of honour! and how much honour
Pick'd from the chaff and ruin of the times   50
To be new-varnish'd!   Well, but to my choice:
'Who chooseth me shall get as much as he deserves.'
I will assume desert.   Give me a key for this,
And instantly unlock my fortunes here.
                        [*He opens the silver casket.*

Portia.   Too long a pause for that which you find there.

Arragon.   What's here? the portrait of a blinking idiot,
Presenting me a schedule! I will read it.

How much unlike art thou to Portia!
How much unlike my hopes and my deservings!
'Who chooseth me shall have as much as he deserves.'   60
Did I deserve no more than a fool's head?
Is that my prize? are my deserts no better?

Portia.   To offend, and judge, are distinct offices
And of opposed natures.

    Arragon.   What is here?

[*Reads*]   "The fire seven times tried this:
    Seven times tried that judgment is,
    That did never choose amiss.
    Some there be that shadows kiss;
    Such have but a shadow's bliss: 70
    There be fools alive, I wis,
    Silver'd o'er; and so was this.
    Take what wife you will to wed,
    I will ever be your head:
    So be gone: you are sped."

Still more fool I shall appear
By the time I linger here:
With one fool's head I came to woo,
But I go away with two.
Sweet, adieu.   I'll keep my oath,   80
Patiently to bear my wroth.

               [*Exeunt Arragon and train.*

Portia.   Thus hath the candle singed the moth.
O, these deliberate fools! when they do choose,
They have the wisdom by their wit to lose.

Nerissa.   The ancient saying is no heresy,
Hanging and wiving goes by destiny.

Portia.   Come, draw the curtain, Nerissa.

Enter a Servant.

Servant.   Where is my lady?

Portia.   Here: what would my lord!

Servant.   Madam, there is alighted at your gate   90
A young Venetian, one that comes before
To signify the approaching of his lord;
From whom he bringeth sensible regreets,
To wit, besides commends and courteous breath,
Gifts of rich value.   Yet I have not seen
So likely an ambassador of love:
A day in April never came so sweet,
To show how costly summer was at hand,
As this fore-spurrer comes before his lord.

Portia.   No more, I pray thee: I am half afeard   100
Thou wilt say anon he is some kin to thee,
Thou spend'st such high-day wit in praising him.
Come, come, Nerissa; for I long to see
Quick Cupid's post that comes so mannerly.

Nerissa.   Bassanio, lord Love, if thy will it be!   [*Exeunt.*

ACT III.

Scene I.   *Venice.   A street.*

Enter Salanio *and* Salarino.

Salanio.   Now, what news on the Rialto?

Salarino.   Why, yet it lives there unchecked that
Antonio hath a ship of rich lading wrecked on the
narrow seas; the Goodwins, I think they call the place;
a very dangerous flat and fatal, where the carcases of
many a tall ship lie buried, as they say, if my gossip
Report be an honest woman of her word.

Salanio. I would she were as lying a gossip in that as ever knapped ginger or made her neighbours believe she wept for the death of a third husband. But it is true, without any slips of prolixity or crossing the plain highway of talk, that the good Antonio, the honest Antonio,——O that I had a title good enough to keep his name company!—

Salarino. Come, the full stop.

Salanio. Ha! what sayst thou? Why, the end is, he hath lost a ship.

Salarino. I would it might prove the end of his losses.

Salanio. Let me say 'amen' betimes, lest the devil cross my prayer, for here he comes in the likeness of a Jew. 22

Enter SHYLOCK.

How now, Shylock! what news among the merchants?

Shylock. You knew, none so well, none so well as you, of my daughter's flight.

Salarino. That's certain; I, for my part, knew the tailor that made the wings she flew withal.

Salanio. And Shylock, for his own part, knew the bird was fledged; and then it is the complexion of them all to leave the dam. 30

Shylock. My own flesh and blood to rebel!

Salarino. There is more difference between thy flesh and hers than between jet and ivory; more between your bloods than there is between red wine and Rhenish. But tell us, do you hear whether Antonio have had any loss at sea or no?

Shylock. There I have another bad match: a bankrupt, a prodigal, who dare scarce show his head on the Rialto: a beggar, that was used to come so smug upon the mart; let him look to his bond: he was wont to call me usurer; let him look to his bond: he was wont to lend money for a Christian courtesy; let him look to his bond.

Salarino. Why, I am sure, if he forfeit, thou wilt not take his flesh: what's that good for?   44

Shylock. To bait fish withal: if it will feed nothing else, it will feed my revenge. He hath disgraced me, and hindered me half a million; laughed at my losses, mocked at my gains, scorned my nation, thwarted my bargains, cooled my friends, heated mine enemies; and what's his reason? I am a Jew. Hath not a Jew eyes? hath not a Jew hands, organs, dimensions, senses, affections, passions? fed with the same food, hurt with the same weapons, subject to the same diseases, healed by the same means, warmed and cooled by the same winter and summer, as a Christian is? If you prick us, do we not bleed? if you tickle us, do we not laugh? if you poison us, do we not die? and if you wrong us, shall we not revenge? If we are like you in the rest, we will resemble you in that. If a Jew wrong a Christian, what is his humility? Revenge. If a Christian wrong a Jew, what should his sufferance be by Christian example? Why, revenge. The villany you teach me, I will execute, and it shall go hard but I will better the instruction.   64

Enter a Servant.

Servant. Gentlemen, my master Antonio is at his house and desires to speak with you both.

Salarino. We have been up and down to seek him.

Enter TUBAL.

Salanio. Here comes another of the tribe: a third cannot be matched, unless the devil himself turn Jew. 69

[*Exeunt Salanio, Salarino, and Servant.*

Shylock. How now, Tubal! what news from Genoa? hast thou found my daughter?

Tubal. I often came where I did hear of her, but cannot find her.

Shylock. Why, there, there, there, there! a diamond gone, cost me two thousand ducats in Frankfort! The curse never fell upon our nation till now; I never felt it till now; two thousand ducats in that; and other precious, precious jewels. I would my daughter were dead at my foot, and the jewels in her ear! would she were hearsed at my foot, and the ducats in her coffin! No news of them? Why, so: and I know not what's spent in the search: why, thou loss upon loss! the thief gone with so much, and so much to find the thief; and no satisfaction, no revenge: nor no ill luck stirring but what lights on my shoulders; no sighs but of my breathing; no tears but of my shedding.

Tubal. Yes, other men have ill luck too: Antonio, as I heard in Genoa,—

Shylock. What, what, what? ill luck, ill luck? 89

Tubal. Hath an argosy cast away, coming from Tripolis.

Shylock. I thank God, I thank God. Is't true, is't true?

Tubal. I spoke with some of the sailors that escaped the wreck.

Shylock. I thank thee, good Tubal: good news, good news! ha, ha! where? in Genoa?

Shylock. "I had it of Leah when I was a bachelor:"

Act III. Scene I.

Tubal.   Your daughter spent in Genoa, as I heard, in one night fourscore ducats.   98

Shylock.   Thou stickest a dagger in me: I shall never see my gold again: fourscore ducats at a sitting! fourscore ducats!

Tubal.   There came divers of Antonio's creditors in my company to Venice, that swear he cannot choose but break

Shylock.   I am very glad of it: I'll plague him; I'll torture him: I am glad of it.

Tubal.   One of them showed me a ring that he had of your daughter for a monkey.   108

Shylock.   Out upon her!   Thou torturest me, Tubal: it was my turquoise; I had it of Leah when I was a bachelor: I would not have given it for a wilderness of monkeys.

Tubal.   But Antonio is certainly undone.

Shylock.   Nay, that's true, that's very true.   Go, Tubal, fee me an officer; bespeak him a fortnight before. I will have the heart of him, if he forfeit; for, were he out of Venice, I can make what merchandise I will. Go, go, Tubal, and meet me at our synagogue; go, good Tubal; at our synagogue, Tubal.   [*Exeunt.*   119

Scene II.   *Belmont.   A room in Portia's house.*

Enter Bassanio, Portia, Gratiano, Nerissa, *and* Attendants.

Portia.   I pray you, tarry: pause a day or two
Before you hazard, for, in choosing wrong,
I lose your company: therefore forbear awhile.
There's something tells me, but it is not love,
I would not lose you; and you know yourself,

Hate counsels not in such a quality.
But lest you should not understand me well,—
And yet a maiden hath no tongue but thought,—
I would detain you here some month or two
Before you venture for me.   I could teach you   10
How to choose right, but I am then forsworn;
So will I never be: so may you miss me;
But if you do, you'll make me wish a sin,
That I had been forsworn.   Beshrew your eyes,
They have o'erlooked me and divided me;
One half of me is yours, the other half yours,
Mine own, I would say; but if mine, then yours,
And so all yours.   O, these naughty times
Put bars between the owners and their rights!
And so, though yours, not yours.   Prove it so,   20
Let fortune go to hell for it, not I,
I speak too long; but 'tis to peize the time,
To eke it and to draw it out in length,
To stay you from election.

  Bassanio.   Let me choose;
For as I am, I live upon the rack.

  Portia.   Upon the rack, Bassanio! then confess
What treason there is mingled with your love.

  Bassanio.   None but that ugly treason of mistrust,
Which makes me fear the enjoying of my love;   30
There may as well be amity and life
'Tween snow and fire, as treason and my love.

  Portia.   Ay, but I fear you speak upon the rack,
Where men enforcèd do speak anything.

  Bassanio.   Promise me life, and I'll confess the truth.

Portia.   Well then, confess and live.

Bassanio.   'Confess' and 'love'
Had been the very sum of my confession:
O happy torment, when my torturer
Doth teach me answers for deliverance!   40
But let me to my fortune and the caskets.

Portia.   Away, then! I am lock'd in one of them
If you do love me, you will find me out.
Nerissa and the rest, stand all aloof.
Let music sound while he doth make his choice;
Then, if he lose, he makes a swan-like end,
Fading in music: that the comparison
May stand more proper, my eye shall be the stream
And watery death-bed for him.   He may win;
And what is music then?   Then music is   50
Even as the flourish when true subjects bow
To a new-crowned monarch: such it is
As are those dulcet sounds in break of day
That creep into the dreaming bridegroom's ear
And summon him to marriage.   Now he goes,
With no less presence, but with much more love,
Than young Alcides, when he did redeem
The virgin tribute paid by howling Troy
To the sea-monster: I stand for sacrifice;
The rest aloof are the Dardanian wives,   60
With bleared visages, come forth to view
The issue of the exploit.   Go, Hercules!
Live thou, I live; with much much more dismay
I view the fight than thou that makest the fray.

Music, whilst BASSANIO *comments on the caskets to himself.*

SONG.

Tell me where is fancy bred,
Or in the heart or in the head?
How begot, how nourished?
    Reply, reply.
  It is engender'd in the eyes,
  With gazing fed; and fancy dies   **70**
  In the cradle where it lies.
    Let us all ring fancy's knell:
    I'll begin it,—Ding, dong, bell.

All.   Ding, dong, bell.

Bas. So may the outward shows be least themselves:
The world is still deceived with ornament.
In law, what plea so tainted and corrupt
But, being season'd with a gracious voice,
Obscures the show of evil?   In religion,
What damned error, but some sober brow   **80**
Will bless it and approve it with a text,
Hiding the grossness with fair ornament?
There is no vice so simple but assumes
Some mark of virtue on his outward parts:
How many cowards, whose hearts are all as false
As stairs of sand, wear yet upon their chins
The beards of Hercules and frowning Mars,
Who, inward search'd, have livers white as milk;
And these assume but valour's excrement
To render them redoubted!   Look on beauty,   **90**
And you shall see 'tis purchased by the weight;
Which therein works a miracle in nature,
Making them lightest that wear most of it:

So are those crisped snaky golden locks
Which make such wanton gambols with the wind,
Upon supposed fairness, often known
To be the dowry of a second head,
The skull that bred them in the sepulchre.
Thus ornament is but the guiled shore
To a most dangerous sea; the beauteous scarf   100
Veiling an Indian beauty; in a word,
The seeming truth which cunning times put on
To entrap the wisest.   Therefore, thou gaudy gold,
Hard food for Midas, I will none of thee;
Nor none of thee, thou pale and common drudge
'Tween man and man: but thou, thou meagre lead,
Which rather threatened than dost promise aught,
Thy paleness moves me more than eloquence;
And here choose I: joy be the consequence!

  Portia. [*Aside*]. How all the other passions fleet to air,
As doubtful thoughts, and rash-embraced despair,   111
And shuddering fear, and green-eyed jealousy!
O love, be moderate; allay thy ecstasy;
In measure rain thy joy; scant this excess.
I feel too much thy blessing: make it less,
For fear I surfeit.

  Bassanio.   What find I here?

                              [*Opening the leaden casket.*

Fair Portia's counterfeit!   What demi-god
Hath come so near creation?   Move these eyes?
Or whether, riding on the balls of mine,   120
Seem they in motion?   Here are sever'd lips,
Parted with sugar breath: so sweet a bar
Should sunder such sweet friends.   Here in her hairs
The painter plays the spider and hath woven

A golden mesh to entrap the hearts of men
Faster than gnats in cobwebs; but her eyes,—
How could he see to do them? having made one,
Methinks it should have power to steal both his
And leave itself unfurnish'd.   Yet look, how far
The substance of my praise doth wrong this shadow 130
In underprizing it, so far this shadow
Doth limp behind the substance.   Here's the scroll,
The continent and summary of my fortune.

[*Reads*] "You that choose not by the view,
        Chance as fair and choose as true!
        Since this fortune falls to you,
        Be content and seek no new.
        If you be well pleased with this
        And hold your fortune for your bliss,
        Turn you where your lady is   140
        And claim her with a loving kiss."

A gentle scroll.   Fair lady, by your leave;
I come by note, to give and to receive.
Like one of two contending in a prize,
That thinks he hath done well in people's eyes,
Hearing applause and universal shout,
Giddy in spirit, still gazing in a doubt
Whether those peals of praise be his or no,
So, thrice-fair lady, stand I, even so;
As doubtful whether what I see be true,   150
Until confirm'd, sign'd, ratified by you.

    Portia.   You see me, Lord Bassanio, where I stand,
Such as I am: though for myself alone
I would not be ambitious in my wish,
To wish myself much better; yet, for you
I would be trebled twenty times myself;

A thousand times more fair, ten thousand times more rich;
That only to stand high in your account.
I might in virtues, beauties, livings, friends,
Exceed account; but the full sum of me   160
In sum of—something, which, to term in gross,
Is an unlesson'd girl, unschool'd, unpractised;
Happy in this, she is not yet so old
But she may learn; happier than this,
She is not bred so dull but she can learn;
Happiest of all is that her gentle spirit
Commits itself to yours to be directed,
As from her lord, her governor, her king.
Myself and what is mine to you and yours
Is now converted: but now I was the lord   170
Of this fair mansion, master of my servants,
Queen o'er myself; and even now, but now,
This house, these servants and this same myself
Are yours, my lord: I give them with this ring;
Which when you part from, lose, or give away,
Let it presage the ruin of your love
And be my vantage to exclaim on you.

   Bassanio.   Madam, you have bereft me of all words,
Only my blood speaks to you in my veins;
And there is such confusion in my powers   180
As, after some oration fairly spoke
By a beloved prince, there doth appear
Among the buzzing pleased multitude;
Where every something, being blent together,
Turns to a wild of nothing, save of joy,
Express'd and not express'd.   But when this ring
Parts from this finger, then parts life from hence:
O, then be bold to say Bassanio's dead!

Nerissa.   My lord and lady, it is now our time,
That have stood by and seen our wishes prosper,   190
To cry, good joy: good joy, my lord and lady!

Gratiano.   My lord Bassanio and my gentle lady,
I wish you all the joy that you can wish;
For I am sure you can wish none from me:
And when your honours mean to solemnize
The bargain of your faith, I do beseech you,
Even at that time I may be married too.

Bassanio.   With all my heart, so thou canst get a wife.

Gratiano.   I thank your lordship, you have got
    me one.   200
My eyes, my lord, can look as swift as yours:
You saw the mistress, I beheld the maid;
You loved, I loved, for intermission
No more pertains to me, my lord, than you.
Your fortune stood upon the casket there,
And so did mine too, as the matter falls;
For wooing here until I sweat again,
And swearing till my very roof was dry
With oaths of love, at last, if promise last,
I got a promise of this fair one here   210
To have her love, provided that your fortune
Achieved her mistress.

Portia.   Is this true, Nerissa?

Nerissa.   Madam, it is, so you stand pleased withal.

Bassanio.   And do you, Gratiano, mean good faith?

Gratiano.   Yes, faith, my lord.

Bassanio.   Our feast shall be much honour'd in your
    marriage.

Gratiano.   But who comes here? Lorenzo and his
    infidel?   220
What, and my old Venetian friend Salerio?

Enter LORENZO, JESSICA, *and* SALERIO, *a messenger from Venice.*

Bassanio.   Lorenzo and Salerio, welcome hither;
If that the youth of my new interest here
Have power to bid you welcome.   By your leave,
I bid my very friends and countrymen,
Sweet Portia, welcome.

Portia.   So do I, my lord:
They are entirely welcome.

Lorenzo.   I thank your honour.   For my part, my lord,
My purpose was not to have seen you here;   230
But meeting with Salerio by the way,
He did intreat me, past all saying nay,
To come with him along.

Salerio.   I did, my lord;
And I have reason for it.   Signor Antonio
Commends him to you   [*Gives Bassanio a letter.*

Bassanio.   Ere I ope his letter,
I pray you, tell me how my good friend doth.

Salerio.   Not sick, my lord, unless it be in mind;
Nor well, unless in mind: his letter there   240
Will show you his estate.

Gratiano.   Nerissa, cheer **yon** stranger; bid her
        welcome.
Your hand, Salerio: what's the news from Venice?
How doth that royal merchant, good Antonio?
I know he will be glad of our success;
We are the Jasons, we have won the fleece.

Salerio.   I would you had won the fleece that he
        hath lost.

Portia.   There are some shrewd contents in yon same
    paper,   251

That steals the colour from Bassanio's cheek:
Some dear friend dead; else nothing in the world
Could turn so much the constitution
Of any constant man.   What, worse and worse!
With leave, Bassanio; I am half yourself,
And I must freely have the half of anything
That this same paper brings you.

   Bassanio.   O sweet Portia,
Here are a few of the unpleasant'st words   260
That ever blotted paper!   Gentle lady,
When I did first impart my love to you,
I freely told you, all the wealth I had
Ran in my veins, I was a gentleman;
And then I told you true: and yet dear lady,
Rating myself at nothing, you shall see
How much I was a braggart.   When I told you
My state was nothing, I should then have told you
That I was worse than nothing; for indeed
I have engaged myself to a dear friend,   270
Engaged my friend to his mere enemy,
To feed my means.   Here is a letter, lady;
The paper as the body of my friend,
And every word in it a gaping wound,
Issuing life-blood.   But is it true, Salerio?
Have all his ventures fail'd?   What, not one hit?
From Tripolis, from Mexico and England,
From Lisbon, Barbary and India?
And not one vessel 'scape the dreadful touch
Of merchant-marring rocks?   280

   Salerio.   Not one, my lord.
Besides, it should appear, that if he had
The present money to discharge the Jew,

He would not take it.   Never did I know
A creature, that did bear the shape of man,
So keen and greedy to confound a man:
He plies the duke at morning and at night,
And doth impeach the freedom of the state,
If they deny him justice: twenty merchants,
The duke himself, and the magnificoes   290
Of greatest port, have all persuaded with him;
But none can drive him from the envious plea
Of forfeiture, of justice and his bond.

Jessica.   When I was with him I have heard him swear
To Tubal and to Chus, his countrymen,
That he would rather have Antonio's flesh
Than twenty times the value of the sum
That he did owe him: and I know, my lord,
If law, authority and power deny not,
It will go hard with poor Antonio.   300

Portia.   Is it your dear friend that is thus in trouble?

Bassanio.   The dearest friend to me, the kindest man,
The best-condition'd and unwearied spirit
In doing courtesies, and one in whom
The ancient Roman honour more appears
Than any that draws breath in Italy.

Portia.   What sum owes he the Jew?

Bassanio.   For me three thousand ducats.

Portia.   What, no more?
Pay him six thousand, and deface the bond;   310
Double six thousand, and then treble that,
Before a friend of this description
Shall lose a hair through Bassanio's fault.
First go with me to church and call me wife,

And then away to Venice to your friend;
For never shall you lie by Portia's side
With an unquiet soul.   You shall have gold
To pay the petty debt twenty times over:
When it is paid, bring your true friend along.
My maid Nerissa and myself meantime   320
Will live as maids and widows.   Come, away!
For you shall hence upon your wedding-day:
Bid your friends welcome, show a merry cheer:
Since you are dear bought, I will love you dear.
But let me hear the letter of your friend.

Bassanio.   [*Reads*] "Sweet Bassanio, my ships have all
miscarried, my creditors grow cruel, my estate is very
low, my bond to the Jew is forfeit; and since in paying
it, it is impossible I should live, all debts are cleared
between you and I, if I might but see you at my death.
Notwithstanding, use your pleasure: if your love do not
persuade you to come, let not my letter."   332

Portia.   O love, dispatch all business, and be gone!

Bassanio.   Since I have your good leave to go away.
I will make haste: but, till I come again,
No bed shall e'er be guilty of my stay,
No rest be interposer 'twixt us twain.   [*Exeunt.*

SCENE III.   *Venice.   A street.*

Enter SHYLOCK, SALARINO, ANTONIO, *and* Gaoler.

Shylock.   Gaoler, look to him: tell not me of mercy;
This is the fool that lent out money gratis:
Gaoler, look to him.

Antonio.   Hear me yet, good Shylock

Shylock.   I'll have my bond; speak not against my
    bond:
I have sworn an oath that I will have my bond.
Thou call'dst me dog before thou hadst a cause;
But, since I am a dog, beware my fangs:
The duke shall grant me justice.   I do wonder,   10
Thou naughty gaoler, that thou art so fond
To come abroad with him at his request.

Antonio.   I pray thee, hear me speak.

Shylock.   I'll have my bond; I will not hear thee speak,
I'll have my bond; and therefore speak no more.
I'll not be made a soft and dull-eyed fool,
To shake the head, relent, and sigh, and yield
To Christian intercessors.   Follow not;
I'll have no speaking; I will have my bond.   [*Exit.*

Salarino.   It is the most impenetrable cur   20
That ever kept with men.

Antonio.   Let him alone:
I'll follow him no more with bootless prayers.
He seeks my life; his reason well I know:
I oft deliver'd from his forfeitures
Many that have at times made moan to me:
Therefore he hates me.

Salarino.   I am sure the duke
Will never grant this forfeiture to hold.

Antonio: The duke cannot deny the course of law: 30
For the commodity that strangers have
With us in Venice, if it be denied,
Will much impeach the justice of his state;
Since that the trade and profit of the city
Consisteth of all nations.   Therefore, go:

These griefs and losses have so bated me,
That I shall hardly spare a pound of flesh
To-morrow to my bloody creditor.
Well, gaoler, on.   Pray God, Bassanio come
To see me pay his debt, and then I care not! [*Exeunt.*   40

SCENE IV.   *Belmont.   A room in Portia's house.*

Enter PORTIA, NERISSA, LORENZO, JESSICA, *and* BALTHASAR.

Lorenzo.   Madam, although I speak it in your presence,
You have a noble and a true conceit
Of god-like amity; which appears most strongly
In bearing thus the absence of your lord.
But if you knew to whom you show this honour,
How true a gentleman you send relief,
How dear a lover of my lord your husband,
I know you would be prouder of the work
Than customary bounty can enforce you.

Portia.   I never did repent for doing good,   10
Nor shall not now: for in companions
That do converse and waste the time together,
Whose souls do bear an equal yoke of love,
There must be needs a like proportion
Of lineaments, of manners and of spirit;
Which makes me think that this Antonio,
Being the bosom lover of my lord,
Must needs be like my lord.   If it be so,
How little is the cost I have bestow'd
In purchasing the semblance of my soul   20
From out the state of hellish misery!
This comes too near the praising of myself:
Therefore no more of it: hear other things.
Lorenzo, I commit into your hands

The husbandry and manage of my house
Until my lord's return: for mine own part,
I have toward heaven breathed a secret vow
To live in prayer and contemplation,
Only attended by Nerissa here,
Until her husband and my lord's return: 30
There is a monastery two miles off:
And there will we abide.   I do desire you
Not to deny this imposition,
The which my love and some necessity
Now lays upon you.

    Lorenzo.   Madam, with all my heart:
I shall obey you in all fair commands.

    Portia.   My people do already know my mind,
And will acknowledge you and Jessica
In place of Lord Bassanio and myself.   40
And so farewell, till we shall meet again.

    Lorenzo.   Fair thoughts and happy hours attend on
        you!

    Jessica.   I wish your ladyship all heart's content.

    Portia.   I thank you for your wish, and am well
        pleased

To wish it back on you: fare you well, Jessica.

                    [Exeunt Jessica and Lorenzo.

Now Balthasar,
As I have ever found thee honest-true,
So let me find thee still.   Take this same letter,   50
And use thou all the endeavour of a man
In speed to Padua! see thou render this
Into my cousin's hand, Doctor Bellario;
And, look, what notes and garments he doth give thee,
Bring them, I pray thee, with imagined speed

Unto the tranect, to the common ferry
Which trades to Venice.   Waste no time in words,
But get thee gone: I shall be there before thee.

   Balthasar.   Madam, I go with all convenient speed.

                                      [Exit.

   Portia.   Come on, Nerissa; I have work in hand   60
That you yet know not of: we'll see our husbands
Before they think of us.

   Nerissa.   Shall they see us?

   Portia.   They shall, Nerissa; but in such a habit,
That they shall think we are accomplished
With that we lack.   I'll hold thee any wager,
When we are both accoutred like young men,
I'll prove the prettier fellow of the two,
And wear my dagger with the braver grace,
And speak between the change of man and boy   70
With a reed voice, and turn two mincing steps
Into a manly stride, and speak of frays
Like a fine bragging youth, and tell quaint lies,
How honourable ladies sought my love,
Which I denying they fell sick and died;
I could not do withal; then I'll repent,
And wish, for all that, that I had not kill'd them;
And twenty of these puny lies I'll tell,
That men shall swear I have discontinued school
Above a twelvemonth.   I have within my mind   80
A thousand raw tricks of these bragging Jacks,
Which I will practise.
But come, I'll tell thee all my whole device
When I am in my coach, which stays for us
At the park gate; and therefore haste away,
For we must measure twenty miles to-day.   *[Exeunt.*

SCENE V. *Tho same. A gardon.*

Enter LAUNCELOT *and* JESSICA.

Launcelot. Yes, truly; for, look you, the sins of the father are to be laid upon the children: therefore, I promise ye, I fear you. I was always plain with you, and so now I speak my agitation of the matter: therefore be of good cheer, for truly I think you are damned. There is but one hope in it that can do you any good; and that is but a kind of base hope neither.

Jessica. And what hope is that, I pray thee?

Launcelot. Marry, you may partly hope that you are not the Jew's daughter.   10

Jessica. That were a kind of base hope, indeed; so the sins of my mother should be visited upon me.

Launcelot. Truly then I fear you are damned both by father and mother: thus when I shun Scylla, your father, I fall into Charybdis, your mother: well, you are gone both ways.

Jessica. I shall be saved by my husband; he hath made me a Christian.

Launcelot. Truly, the more to blame he: we were Christians enow before; e'en as many as could well live, one by another. This making of Christians will raise the price of hogs: if we grow all to be pork-eaters, we shall not shortly have a rasher on the coals for money.

Enter LORENZO.

Jessica. I'll tell my husband, Launcelot, what you say: here he comes   25

Lorenzo. I shall grow jealous of you shortly, **Launcelot.**

Jessica.   Nay, you need not fear us, Lorenzo: Launcelot and I are out. He tells me flatly, there is no mercy
for me in heaven, because I am a Jew's daughter: and
he says, you are no good member of the commonwealth,
for in converting Jews to Christians, you raise the price
of pork.

Lorenzo.   I think the best grace of wit will shortly
turn into silence, and discourse grow commendable in
none only but parrots.   Go in, sirrah: bid them prepare
for dinner.

Launcelot.   That is done, sir; they have all stomachs.

Lorenzo.   Goodly Lord, what a wit-snapper are you!
then bid them prepare dinner.   40

Launcelot.   That is done too, sir; only 'cover' is the
word.

Lorenzo.   Will you cover then, sir?

Launcelot.   Not so, sir, neither; I know my duty.

Lorenzo.   Yet more quarrelling with occasion! Wilt
thou show the whole wealth of thy wit in an instant? I
pray thee, understand a plain man in his plain meaning:
go to thy fellows; bid them cover the table, serve in the
meat, and we will come in to dinner.

Launcelot.   For the table, sir, it shall be served in;
for the meat, sir, it shall be covered; for your coming
in to dinner, sir, why, let it be as humours and conceits
shall govern.   [*Exit.*

Lorenzo.   O dear discretion, how his words are suited!
The fool hath planted in his memory   55
An army of good words; and I do know
A many fools, that stand in better place,
Garnish'd like him, that for a tricksy word

Defy the matter.   How cheer'st thou, Jessica?
And now, good sweet, say thy opinion,
How doest thou like the Lord Bassanio's wife?   60

   Jessica.   Past all expressing.   It is very meet
The Lord Bassanio live an upright life;
For, having such a blessing in his lady,
He finds the joys of heaven here on earth;
And if on earth he do not mean it, then
In reason he should never come to heaven.
Why, if two gods should play some heavenly match
And on the wager lay two earthly women,
And Portia one, there must be something else   70
Pawn'd with the other, for the poor rude world
Hath not her fellow.
   Lorenzo.   Even such a husband
Hast thou of me as she is for a wife.
   Jessica.   Nay, but ask my opinion too of that.
   Lorenzo.   I will anon: first let us go to dinner.
   Jessica.   Nay, let me praise you while I have a stomach.
   Lorenzo.   No, pray thee, let it serve for table-talk;
Then, howsoe'er thou speak'st, 'mong other things
I shall digest it.   80
   Jessica.   Well, I'll set you forth.   [*Exeunt.*

ACT IV.

SCENE I.   *Venice.   A court of justice.*

Enter the DUKE, *the* Magnificoes, ANTONIO, BASSANIO, GRATIANO,
SALERIO, *and others.*

   Duke.   What, is Antonio here?
   Antonio.   Ready, so please your grace.
   Duke.   I am sorry for thee: thou art come to answer
A stony adversary, an inhuman wretch

Uncapable of pity, void and empty
From any dram of mercy.

   Antonio.   I have heard
Your grace hath ta'en great pains to qualify
His rigorous course; but since he stands obdurate
And that no lawful means can carry me
Out of his envy's reach, I do oppose   10
My patience to his fury, and am arm'd
To suffer, with a quietness of spirit,
The very tyranny and rage of his.

   Duke.   Go one, and call the Jew into court.

   Salerio.   He is ready at the door: he comes, my lord.

Enter SHYLOCK.

   Duke.   Make room, and let him stand before our face.
Shylock, the world thinks, and I think so too,
That thou but lead'st this fashion of thy malice
To the last hour of act; and then 'tis thought
Thou'lt show thy mercy and remorse more strange   20
Than is thy strange apparent cruelty;
And where thou now exact'st the penalty,
Which is a pound of this poor merchant's flesh,
Thou wilt not only loose the forfeiture,
But, touch'd with human gentleness and love,
Forgive a moiety of the principal;
Glancing an eye of pity on his losses,
That have of late so huddled on his back,
Enow to press a royal merchant down
And pluck commiseration of his state   30
From brassy bosoms and rough hearts of flint,
From stubborn Turks and Tartars, never train'd

To offices of tender courtesy.
We all expect a gentle answer, Jew.

Shylock. I have possess'd your grace of what I purpose
And by our holy Sabbath have I sworn
To have the due and forfeit of my bond:
If you deny it, let the danger light
Upon your charter and your city's freedom.
You'll ask me, why I rather choose to have   40
A weight of carrion flesh than to receive
Three thousand ducats: I'll not answer that;
But, say, it is my humour: is it answer'd?
What if my house be troubled with a rat,
And I be pleased to give ten thousand ducats
To have it baned?   What, are you answer'd yet?
Some men there are love not a gaping pig;
Some, that are mad if they behold a cat;
Some, when they hear the bagpipe: for affection,
Mistress of passion, sways it to the mood   50
Of what it likes or loathes.   Now, for your answer:
As there is no firm reason to be render'd,
Why he cannot abide a gaping pig;
Why he, a harmless necessary cat;
Why he, a woollen bag-pipe; but of force
Must yield to such inevitable shame
As to offend, himself being offended;
So can I give no reason, nor I will not,
More than a lodged hate and a certain loathing
I bear Antonio, that I follow thus   60
A losing suit against him.   Are you answer'd?

Bassanio. This is no answer, thou unfeeling man,
To excuse the current of thy cruelty.

Shylock. I am not bound to please thee with my
answers.

Bassanio. Do all men kill the things they do not love?

Shylock. Hates any man the thing he would not kill?

Bassanio. Every offence is not a hate at first.

Shylock. What, wouldst thou have a serpent sting
thee twice?   70

Antonio. I pray you, think you question with the
Jew:

You may as well go stand upon the beach
And bid the main flood bate his usual height;
You may as well use question with the wolf
Why he hath made the ewe bleat for the lamb;
You may as well forbid the mountain pines
To wag their high tops and to make no noise,
When they are fretten with the gusts of heaven;
You may as well do anything most hard,   80
As seek to soften that—than which what's harder?—
His Jewish heart: therefore, I do beseech you,
Make no more offers, use no farther means,
But with all brief and plain conveniency
Let me have judgment and the Jew his will.

Bassanio. For thy three thousand ducats here is six.

Shylock. If every ducat in six thousand ducats
Were in six parts and every part a ducat,
I would not draw them; I would have my bond.

Duke. How shalt thou hope for mercy, rendering
none?   91

Shylock. What judgment shall I dread, doing no
wrong?

You have among you many a purchased slave,

Which, like your asses and your dogs and mules,
You use in abject and in slavish parts,
Because you bought them: shall I say to you,
Let them be free, marry them to your heirs?
Why sweat they under burthens? let their beds
Be made as soft as yours and let their palates   100
Be season'd with such viands?   You will answer
'The slaves are ours:' so do I answer you:
The pound of flesh, which I demand of him,
Is dearly bought; 'tis mine and I will have it.
If you deny me, fie upon your law!
There is no force in the decrees of Venice.
I stand for judgment: answer; shall I have it?

Duke.   Upon my power I may dismiss this court,
Unless Ballario, a learned doctor,
Whom I have sent for to determine this,   110
Come here to-day.

Salerio.   My lord, here stays without
A messenger with letters from the doctor,
New come from Padua.

Duke.   Bring us letters; call the messenger.

Bassanio.   Good cheer, Antonio! What, man, courage
       yet!
The Jew shall have my flesh, blood, bones, and all,
Ere thou shalt lose for me one drop of blood.

Antonio.   I am a tainted wether of the flock,   120
Meetest for death: the weakest kind of fruit
Drops earliest to the ground; and so let me:
You cannot better be employ'd, Bassanio,
Than to live still and write mine epitaph.

Enter NERISSA, *dressed like a lawyer's clerk.*

Duke.   Came you from Padua, from Bellario?

Nerissa.   From both, my lord.   Bellario greets your
grace.

[*Presenting a letter.*

Bassanio.   Why dost thou whet thy knife so earnestly?

Shylock.   To cut the forfeiture from that bankrupt
there   130

Gratiano.   Not on thy sole, but on thy soul, harsh Jew,
Thou makest thy knife keen; but no metal can,
No, not the hangman's axe, bear half the keenness
Of thy sharp envy.   Can no prayers pierce thee?

Shylock.   No, none that thou has wit enough to make.

Gratiano.   O, be thou damn'd, inexorable dog!
And for thy life let justice be accused.
Thou almost makest me waver in my faith
To hold opinion with Pythagoras,
That souls of animals infuse themselves   140
Into the trunks of men: thy currish spirit
Govern'd a wolf, who, hang'd for human slaughter,
Even from the gallows did his fell soul fleet,
And, whilst thou lay'st in thy unhallow'd dam,
Infused itself in thee; for thy desires
Are wolfish, bloody, starved and ravenous.

Shylock.   Till thou canst rail the seal from off my bond,
Thou but offend'st thy lungs to speak so loud:
Repair thy wit, good youth, or it will fall
To cureless ruin.   I stand here for law.   150

Duke.   This letter from Bellario doth commend
A young and learned doctor to our court.
Where is he?

Nerissa.   He attendeth here hard by,
To know your answer, whether you'll admit him.

Duke.   With all my heart.   Some three or four of you
Go give him courteous conduct to this place.
Meantime the court shall hear Bellario's letter.   158

Clerk.   [*Reads*] "Your grace shall understand that at the
receipt of your letter I am very sick: but in the instant
that your messenger came, in loving visitation was with
me a young doctor of Rome; his name is Balthasar.   I
acquainted him with the cause in controversy between
the Jew and Antonio the merchant: we turned o'er
many books together: he is furnished with my opinion;
which, bettered with his own learning, the greatness
whereof I cannot enough commend, comes with him, at
my importunity, to fill up your grace's request in my
stead.   I beseech you, let his lack of years be no im-
pediment to let him lack a reverend estimation; for I
never knew so young a body with so old a head.   I leave
him to your gracious acceptance, whose trial shall better
publish his commendation."

Duke.   You hear the learn'd Bellario, what he writes:
And here, I take it, is the doctor come.   175

Enter PORTIA, *dressed like a doctor of laws.*

Give me your hand.   Come you from old Bellario?

Portia.   I did, my lord.

Duke.   You are welcome: take your place.
Are you acquainted with the difference
That holds this present question in the court?   180

Portia.   I am informed throughly of the cause.
Which is the merchant here, and which the Jew?

Duke.   Antonio and old Shylock, both stand forth.

Portia.   Is your name Shylock?

Shylock.   Shylock is my name

Portia.   Of a strange nature is the suit you follow;
Yet in such rule that the Venetian law
Cannot impugn you as you do proceed.
You stand within his danger, do you not?

Antonio.   Ay, so he says.   190

Portia.   Do you confess the bond?

Antonio.   I do.

Portia.   Then must the Jew be merciful.

Shylock.   On what compulsion must I? tell me that.

Portia.   The quality of mercy is not strain'd,
It droppeth as the gentle rain from heaven
Upon the place beneath; it is twice blest;
It blesseth him that gives and him that takes:
'Tis mightiest in the mightiest: it becomes
The throned monarch better than his crown;   200
His sceptre shows the force of temporal power,
The attribute to awe and majesty,
Wherein doth sit the dread and fear of kings;
But mercy is above this sceptred sway;
It is enthroned in the hearts of kings,
It is an attribute to God himself;
And earthly power doth then show likest God's
When mercy seasons justice.   Therefore, Jew,
Though justice be thy plea, consider this,
That, in the course of justice, none of us   210
Should see salvation: we do pray for mercy;
And that same prayer doth teach us all to render
The deeds of mercy.   I have spoke thus much

Shylock. "A Daniel come to judgment!"

Act IV. Scene I

To mitigate the justice of thy plea;
Which if thou follow, this strict court of Venice
Must needs give sentence 'gainst the merchant there.

Shylock.   My deeds upon my head! I crave the law,
The penalty and forfeit of my bond.

Portia.   Is he not able to discharge the money?

Bassanio.   Yes, here I tender it for him in the court;
Yea, twice the sum: if that will not suffice,   221
I will be bound to pay it ten times o'er,
On forfeit of my hands, my head, my heart:
If this will not suffice, it must appear
That malice bears down truth.   And I beseech you,
Wrest once the law to your authority:
To do a great right, do a little wrong,
And curb this cruel devil of his will.

Portia.   It must not be; there is no power in Venice
Can alter a decree established: 230
'Twill be recorded for a precedent,
And many an error by the same example
Will rush into the state: it cannot be.

Shylock.   A Daniel come to judgment! yea, a Daniel!
O wise young judge, how I do honour thee!

Portia.   I pray you, let me look upon the bond.

Shylock.   Here 'tis, most reverend doctor, here it is.

Portia.   Shylock, there's thrice thy money offer'd thee.

Shylock.   An oath, an oath, I have an oath in heaven:
Shall I lay perjury upon my soul?   240
No, not for Venice.

Portia.   Why, this bond is forfeit;
And lawfully by this the Jew may claim
A pound of flesh, to be by him cut off

Nearest the merchant's heart.   Be merciful:
Take thrice thy money; bid me tear the bond.

Shylock.   When it is paid according to the tenour.
It doth appear you are a worthy judge;
You know the law, your exposition
Hath been most sound: I charge you by the law,   250
Whereof you are a well-deserving pillar,
Proceed to judgment: by my soul I swear
There is no power in the tongue of man
To alter me: I stay here on my bond.

Antonio.   Most heartily I do beseech the court
To give the judgment.

Portia.   Why then, thus it is:
You must prepare your bosom for his knife.

Shylock.   O noble judge! O excellent young man!

Portia.   For the intent and purpose of the law   260
Hath full relation to the penalty
Which here appeareth due upon the bond.

Shylock.   'Tis very true: O wise and upright judge!
How much more elder art thou than thy looks!

Portia.   Therefore lay bare your bosom.

Shylock.   Ay, his breast:
So says the bond: doth it not, noble judge?
'Nearest his heart;' those are the very words.

Portia.   It is so.   Are there balance here to weigh
The flesh?   270

Shylock.   I have them ready.

Portia.   Have by some surgeon, Shylock, on your
        charge,
To stop his wounds, lest he do bleed to death.

Shylock.   Is it so nominated in the bond?

Portia.   It is not so express'd: but what of that?
'Twere good you do so much for charity.

Shylock.   I cannot find it; 'tis not in the bond.

Portia.   You, merchant, have you anything to say?

Antonio.   But little: I am arm'd and well prepared.
Give me your hand, Bassanio: fare you well!   281
Grieve not that I am fallen to this for you;
For herein Fortune shows herself more kind
Than is her custom: it is still her use
To let the wretched man outlive his wealth,
To view with hollow eye and wrinkled brow
An age of poverty; from which lingering penance
Of such misery doth she cut me off.
Commend me to your honourable wife:
Tell her the process of Antonio's end;   290
Say how I loved you, speak me fair in death;
And, when the tale is told, bid her be judge
Whether Bassanio had not once a love.
Repent but you that you shall lose your friend,
And he repents not that he pays your debt;
For if the Jew do cut but deep enough.
I'll pay it presently with all my heart.

Bassanio.   Antonio, I am married to a wife
Which is as dear to me as life itself;
But life itself, my wife, and all the world,   300
Are not with me esteem'd above thy life:
I would lose all, ay, sacrifice them all
Here to this devil, to deliver you.

Portia.   Your wife would give you little thanks for
        that,
If she were by, to hear you make the offer.

Gratiano. I have a wife, whom, I protest, I love:
I would she were in heaven, so she could
Entreat some power to change this currish Jew.

Nerissa. 'Tis well you offer it behind her back;   310
The wish would make else an unquiet house.

Shylock. [*Aside*] These be the Christian husbands. I
        have a daughter;
Would any of the stock of Barrabas
Had been her husband rather than a Christian!
[*Aloud*] We trifle time: I pray thee, pursue sentence.

Portia. A pound of that same merchant's flesh is
        thine:
The court awards it, and the law doth give it.

Shylock. Most rightful judge!   320

Portia. And you must cut this flesh from off his
        breast:
The law allows it, and the court awards it.

Shylock. Most learned judge! A sentence! Come,
        prepare!

Portia. Tarry a little; there is something else.
This bond doth give thee here no jot of blood;
The words expressly are 'a pound of flesh:'
Take then thy bond, take thou thy pound of flesh;
But, in the cutting it, if thou dost shed   330
One drop of Christian blood, thy lands and goods
Are, by the laws of Venice, confiscate
Unto the state of Venice.

Gratiano. O upright judge! Mark, Jew: O learned
        judge!

Shylock. Is that the law?

Portia.   Thyself shalt see the act;
For, as thou urgest justice, be assured
Thou shalt have justice, more than thou desirest.

Gratiano.   O learned judge! Mark, Jew: a learned
    judge!   341

Shylock.   I take this offer, then; pay the bond thrice
And let the Christian go.

Bassanio.   Here is the money.

Portia.   Soft!
The Jew shall have all justice; soft! no haste:
He shall have nothing but the penalty.

Gratiano.   O Jew! an upright judge, a learned judge!

Portia.   Therefore prepare thee to cut off the flesh.
Shed thou no blood, nor cut thou less nor more   35
But just a pound of flesh: if thou cut'st more
Or less than a just pound, be it but so much
As makes it light or heavy in the substance,
Or the division of the twentieth part
Of one poor scruple, nay, if the scale do turn
But in the estimation of a hair,
Thou diest and all thy goods are confiscate.

Gratiano.   A second Daniel, a Daniel, Jew!
Now, infidel, I have thee on the hip.

Portia.   What doth the Jew pause? take thy forfeiture.

Shylock.   Give me my principal, and let me go.   361

Bassanio.   I have it ready for thee; here it is.

Portia.   He hath refused it in the open court:
He shall have merely justice and his bond.

Gratiano.   A Daniel, still say I, a second Daniel!
I thank thee, Jew, for teaching me that word.

Shylock.   Shall I not have barely my principal?

Portia.   Thou shalt have nothing but the forfeiture,
To be so taken at thy peril, Jew.

Shylock.   Why, then the devil give him good of it!   370
I'll stay no longer question.

Portia.   Tarry, Jew:
The law hath yet another hold on you.
It is enacted in the laws of Venice,
If it be proved against an alien
That by direct or indirect attempts
He seek the life of any citizen,
The party 'gainst the which he doth contrive
Shall seize one half his goods; the other half
Comes to the privy coffer of the state;   380
And the offender's life lies in the mercy
Of the duke only, 'gainst all other voice.
In which predicament, I say, thou stand'st;
For it appears, by manifest proceeding,
That indirectly and directly too
Thou hast contrived against the very life
Of the defendant; and thou hast incurr'd
The danger formerly by me rehearsed.
Down therefore and beg mercy of the duke.

Gratiano.   Beg that thou mayst have leave to hang
          thyself: 391
And yet, thy wealth being forfeit to the state,
Thou hast not left the value of a cord;
Therefore thou must be hang'd at the state's charge.

Duke.   That thou shalt see the difference of our spirits,
I pardon thee thy life before thou ask it:
For half thy wealth, it is Antonio's;

The other half comes to the general state,
Which humbleness may drive unto a fine.

Portia.   Ay, for the state, not for Antonio.   400

Shylock.   Nay, take my life and all; pardon not that:
You take my house when you do take the prop
That doth sustain my house; you take my life
When you do take the means whereby I live.

Portia.   What mercy can you render him, Antonio?

Gratiano.   A halter gratis; nothing else, for God's
    sake.

Antonio.   So please my lord the duke and all the court
To quit the fine for one half of his goods,
I am content; so he will let me have   410
The other half in use, to render it,
Upon his death, unto the gentleman
That lately stole his daughter:
Two things provided more, that, for this favour,
He presently become a Christian;
The other, that he do record a gift,
Here in the court, of all he dies possess'd,
Unto his son Lorenzo and his daughter.

Duke.   He shall do this, or else I do recant
The pardon that I late pronounced here.   420

Portia.   Art thou contented, Jew? what dost thou say?

Shylock.   I am content.

Portia.   Clerk, draw a deed of gift.

Shylock.   I pray you, give me leave to go from hence;
I am not well: send the deed after me,
And I will sign it.

Duke.   Get thee gone, but do it.

Gratiano.   In christening shalt thou have two god-
        fathers
Had I been judge, thou shouldst have had ten more,   430
To bring thee to the gallows, not the font.   [*Exit Shylock.*

Duke.   Sir, I entreat you home with me to dinner.

Portia.   I humbly do desire your grace of pardon:
I must away this night toward Padua,
And it is meet I presently set forth.

Duke.   I am sorry that your leisure serves you not.
Antonio, gratify this gentleman,
For, in my mind, you are much bound to him.

                    [*Exeunt Duke and his train.*

Bassanio.   Most worthy gentleman, I and my friend
Have by your wisdom been this day acquitted   440
Of grievous penalties; in lieu whereof,
Three thousand ducats, due unto the Jew,
We freely cope your courteous pains withal.

Antonio.   And stand indebted, over and above,
In love and service to you evermore.

Portia.   He is well paid that is well satisfied;
And I, delivering you, am satisfied
And therein do account myself well paid:
My mind was never yet more mercenary.
I pray you, know me when we meet again: 450
I wish you well, and so I take my leave.

Bassanio.   Dear sir, of force I must attempt you
        further:
Take some remembrance of us, as a tribute,
Not as a fee: grant me two things, I pray you,
Not to deny me, and to pardon me.

Portia.   You press me far, and therefore I will yield.

[*To Antonio*] Give me your gloves, I'll wear them for
    your sake;

[*To Bassanio*] And, for your love, I'll take this ring from
    you: 461

Do not draw back your hand; I'll take no more;

And you in love shall not deny me this.

    Bassanio.   This ring, good sir, alas, it is a trifle!

I will not shame myself to give you this.

    Portia.   I will have nothing else but only this,

And now methinks I have a mind to it.

    Bassanio.   There's more depends on this than on the
    value.

The dearest ring in Venice will I give you,   470

And find it out by proclamation:

Only for this, I pray you, pardon me.

    Portia.   I see, sir, you are liberal in offers:

You taught me first to beg; and now methinks

You teach me how a beggar should be answer'd.

    Bassanio.   Good sir, this ring was given me by my
    wife;

And when she put it on, she made me vow

That I should neither sell nor give nor lose it.

    Portia.   That 'scuse serves many men to save their
    gifts.   481

An if your wife be not a mad-woman,

And know how well I have deserved the ring,

She would not hold out enemy for ever,

For giving it to me.   Well, peace be with you!

                           [*Exeunt Portia and Nerissa.*

    Antonio.   My Lord Bassanio, let him have the ring:

Let his deservings and my love withal

Be valued 'gainst your wife's commandment.

Bassanio.   Go, Gratiano, run and overtake him;
Give him the ring, and bring him, if thou canst,   490
Unto Antonio's house: away! make haste.   [*Exit Gratiano.*
Come, you and I will thither presently;
And in the morning early will we both
Fly toward Belmont: come, Antonio.   [*Exeunt.*

SCENE II.   *The same.   A street.*

Enter PORTIA *and* NERISSA.

Portia.   Inquire the Jew's house out, give him this
      deed
And let him sign it: we'll away to-night
And be a day before our husbands home:
This deed will be well welcome to Lorenzo.

Enter GRATIANO.

Gratiano.   Fair sir, you are well o'erta'en:
My Lord Bassanio upon more advice
Hath sent you here this ring, and doth entreat
Your company at dinner.

Portia.   That cannot be: 10
His ring I do accept most thankfully:
And so, I pray you, tell him: furthermore,
I pray you, show my youth old Shylock's house.

Gratiano.   That will I do.

Nerissa.   Sir, I would speak with you
[*Aside to Portia*] I'll see if I can get my husband's ring,
Which I did make him swear to keep for ever.

Portia. [*Aside to Nerissa*] Thou may'st, I warrant.   We
      shall have old swearing
That they did give the rings away to men;   20

But we'll outface them, and outswear them too.

[*Aloud*] Away! make haste: thou know'st where I will
   tarry.

   Nerissa.   Come, good sir, will you shew me to this
   house?   [*Exeunt.*

ACT V

SCENE I.   *Belmont.   Avenue to Portia's house.*

Enter LORENZO *and* JESSICA.

   Lorenzo.   The moon shines bright: in such a night as
      this,
When the sweet wind did gently kiss the trees
And they did make no noise, in such a night
Troilus methinks mounted the Troyan walls
And sigh'd his soul toward the Grecian tents,
Where Cressid lay that night.

   Jessica.   In such a night
Did Thisbe fearfully o'ertrip the dew
And saw the lion's shadow ere himself   10
And ran dismay'd away.

   Lorenzo.   In such a night
Stood Dido with a willow in her hand
Upon the wild sea banks and waft her love
To come again to Carthage.

   Jessica.   In such a night
Medea gather'd the enchanted herbs
That did renew old Æson.

   Lorenzo.   In such a night
Did Jessica steal from the wealthy Jew   20
And with an unthrift love did run from Venice
As far as Belmont.

Jessica.   In such a night
Did young Lorenzo swear he loved her well,
Stealing her soul with many vows of faith
And ne'er a true one.

Lorenzo.   In such a night
Did pretty Jessica, like a little shrew,
Slander her love, and he forgave it her.

Jessica.   I would out-night you, did no body come; 30
But, hark, I hear the footing of a man.

Enter STEPHANO.

Lorenzo.   Who comes so fast in silence of the night?

Stephano.   A friend.

Lorenzo.   A friend! what friend? your name, I pray
    you, friend?

Stephano.   Stephano is my name; and I bring word
My mistress will before the break of day
Be here at Belmont: she doth stray about
By holy crosses, where she kneels and prays
For happy wedlock hours.   40

Lorenzo.   Who comes with her?

Stephano.   None but a holy hermit and her maid.
I pray you, is my master yet return'd?

Lorenzo.   He is not, nor we have not heard from him.
But go we in, I pray thee, Jessica,
And ceremoniously let us prepare
Some welcome for the mistress of the house.

Enter LAUNCELOT.

Launcelot.   Sola, sola! wo ha, ho! sola, sola!

Lorenzo.   Who calls?

Launcelot.   Sola! did you see Master Lorenzo? Master
Lorenzo, sola, sola!   51

Lorenzo.   Leave hollaing, man: here.

Launcelot.   Sola! where? where?

Lorenzo.   Here.

Launcelot.   Tell him there's a post come from my
master, with his horn full of good news: my master
will be here ere morning.   [*Exit.*

Lorenzo.   Sweet soul, let's in, and there expect their
           coming.
And yet no matter: why should we go in?   60
My friend Stephano, signify, I pray you,
Within the house, your mistress is at hand;
And bring your music forth into the air.   [*Exit Stephano.*
How sweet the moonlight sleeps upon this bank!
Here will we sit and let the sounds of music
Creep in our ears: soft stillness and the night
Become the touches of sweet harmony.
Sit, Jessica.   Look how the floor of heaven
Is thick inlaid with patines of bright gold:
There's not the smallest orb which thou behold'st   70
But in his motion like an angel sings,
Still quiring to the young-eyed cherubins;
Such harmony is in immortal souls;
But whilst this muddy vesture of decay
Doth grossly close it in, we cannot hear it.

Enter Musicians.

Come, ho! and wake Diana with a hymn:
With sweetest touches pierce your mistress' ear
And draw her home with music.   [*Music.*

Jessica.   I am never merry when I hear sweet music.

Lorenzo.   The reason is, your spirits are attentive: 80
For do but note a wild and wanton herd,
Or race of youthful and unhandled colts,
Fetching mad bounds, bellowing and neighing loud,
Which is the hot condition of their blood;
If they but hear perchance a trumpet sound,
Or any air of music touch their ears,
You shall perceive them make a mutual stand,
Their savage eyes turn'd to a modest gaze
By the sweet power of music; therefore the poet
Did feign that Orpheus drew trees, stones and floods;   90
Since nought so stockish, hard and full of rage,
But music for the time doth change his nature.
The man that hath no music in himself,
Nor is not moved with concord of sweet sounds,
Is fit for treasons, stratagems and spoils;
The motions of his spirit are dull as night
And his affections dark as Erebus:
Let no such man be trusted.   Mark the music

Enter PORTIA *and* NERISSA.

Portia.   That light we see is burning in my hall.
How far that little candle throws his beams!   100
So shines a good deed in a naughty world.

Nerissa.   When the moon shone, we did not see the
candle.

Portia.   So doth the greater glory dim the less:
A substitute shines brightly as a king
Until a king be by, and then his state
Empties itself, as doth an inland brook
Into the main of waters.   Music! hark!

Lorenzo. "Dear lady, welcome home."

Act V. Scene

Nerissa.   It is your music, madam, of the house.

Portia.   Nothing is good, I see, without respect: 110
Methinks it sounds much sweeter than by day.

Nerissa.   Silence bestows that virtue on it madam.

Portia.   The crow doth sing as sweetly as the lark
When neither is attended, and I think
The nightingale, if she should sing by day,
When every goose is cackling, would be thought
No better a musician than the wren.
How many things by season season'd are
To their right praise and true perfection!
Peace, ho! the moon sleeps with Endymion   120
And would not be awaked.   [*Music ceases.*

Lorenzo.   That is the voice,
Or I am much deceived, of Portia.

Portia.   He knows me as the blind man knows the
            cuckoo,
By the bad voice.

Lorenzo.   Dear lady, welcome home.

Portia.   We have been praying for our husbands'
            healths,
Which speed, we hope, the better for our words.   130
Are they return'd?

Lorenzo.   Madam, they are not yet;
But there is come a messenger before,
To signify their coming.

Portia.   Go in, Nerissa;
Give order to my servants that they take
No note at all of our being absent hence;
Nor you, Lorenzo; Jessica, nor you.   [*A tucket sounds.*

Lorenzo.   Your husband is at hand; I hear his
  trumpet;   140
We are no tell-tales, madam; fear you not.

Portia.   This night methinks is but the daylight sick;
It looks a little paler: 'tis a day,
Such as the day is when the sun is hid.

  Enter BASSANIO, ANTONIO, GRATIANO, *and their followers.*

Bassanio.   We should hold day with the Antipodes,
If you would walk in absence of the sun.

Portia.   Let me give light, but let me not be light;
For a light wife doth make a heavy husband,
And never be Bassanio so for me:
But God sort all! You are welcome home, my lord.   150

Bassanio.   I thank you, madam.   Give welcome to
  my friend.
This is the man, this is Antonio,
To whom I am so infinitely bound.

Portia.   You should in all sense be much bound to him.
For, as I hear, he was much bound for you.

Antonio.   No more than I am well acquitted of.

Portia.   Sir, you are very welcome to our house:
It must appear in other ways than words,
Therefore I scant this breathing courtesy.   160

Gratiano.   [*To Nerissa*]   By yonder moon I swear you
  do me wrong;
In faith, I gave it to the judge's clerk:
Would he were dead that had it, for my part,
Since you do take it, love, so much at heart.

Portia.   A quarrel, ho, already! what's the matter?

Gratiano.   About a hoop of gold, a paltry ring
That she did give me, whose posy was

For all the world like cutler's poetry
Upon a knife, 'Love me, and leave me not.'   170

 Nerissa. What talk you of the posy or the value?
You swore to me, when I did give it you,
That you would wear it till your hour of death
And that it should lie with you in your grave:
Though not for me, yet for your vehement oaths,
You should have been respective and have kept it.
Gave it a judge's clerk! no, God's my judge,
The clerk will ne'er wear hair on's face that had it.

 Gratiano. He will, an if he live to be a man.

 Nerissa. Ay, if a woman live to be a man.   180

 Gratiano. Now, by this hand, I gave it to a youth,
A kind of boy, a little scrubbed boy,
No higher than thyself, the judge's clerk,
A prating boy, that begg'd it as a fee:
I could not for my heart deny it him.

 Portia. You were to blame, I must be plain with you,
To part so slightly with your wife's first gift;
A thing stuck on with oaths upon your finger
And so riveted with faith unto your flesh.
I gave my love a ring and made him swear   190
Never to part with it; and here he stands;
I dare be sworn for him he would not leave it
Nor pluck it from his finger, for the wealth
That the world masters.   Now, in faith, Gratiano,
You give your wife too unkind a cause of grief:
An 'twere to me, I should be mad at it.

 Bassanio. [*Aside*]   Why, I were best to cut my left
  hand off
And swear I lost the ring defending it.

Gratiano.   My Lord Bassanio gave his ring away   200
Unto the judge that begg'd it and indeed
Deserved it too; and then the boy, his clerk,
That took some pains in writing, he begg'd mine;
And neither man nor master would take aught
But the two rings.

Portia.   What ring gave you, my lord?
Not that, I hope, which you received of me.

Bassanio.   If I could add a lie unto a fault,
I would deny it; but you see my finger
Hath not the ring upon it; it is gone.   210

Portia.   Even so void is your false heart of truth.
By heaven, I will never be your wife
Until I see the ring.

Nerissa.   No, nor I yours
Till I again see mine.

Bassanio.   Sweet Portia,
If you did know to whom I gave the ring,
If you did know for whom I gave the ring,
And would conceive for what I gave the ring,
And how unwillingly I left the ring,   220
When nought would be accepted but the ring,
You would abate the strength of your displeasure.

Portia.   If you had known the virtue of the ring,
Or half her worthiness that gave the ring,
Or your own honour to contain the ring,
You would not then have parted with the ring.
What man is there so much unreasonable,
If you had pleased to have defended it
With any terms of zeal, wanted the modesty
To urge the thing held as a ceremony?   230

Nerissa teaches me what to believe:
I'll die for't but some woman had the ring.

Bassanio.   No, by my honour, madam, by my soul,
No woman had it, but a civil doctor,
Which did refuse three thousand ducats of me
And begg'd the ring; the which I did deny him
And suffer'd him to go displeased away;
Even he that did uphold the very life
Of my dear friend.   What should I say, sweet lady?
I was enforced to send it after him;   240
I was beset with shame and courtesy;
My honour would not let ingratitude
So much besmear it.   Pardon me, good lady;
For, by these blessed candles of the night,
Had you been there, I think you would have begg'd
The ring of me to give the worthy doctor.

Portia.   Let not that doctor e'er come near my house:
Since he hath got the jewel that I loved,
And that which you did swear to keep for me,
I will be come as liberal as you;   250
I'll not deny him any thing I have.

Nerissa.   Nor I his clerk; therefore be well advised
How you do leave me to mine own protection.

Antonio.   I am the unhappy subject of these quarrels.

Portia.   Sir, grieve not you; you are welcome not-
    withstanding.

Bassanio.   Portia, forgive me this enforced wrong;
And, in the hearing of these many friends,
I swear to thee, even by thine own fair eyes,
Wherein I see myself—   260

Portia.   Mark you but that!
In both my eyes he doubly sees himself;

In each eye, one: swear by your double self,
And there's an oath of credit.

Bassanio.   Nay, but hear me:
Pardon this fault, and by my soul I swear
I never more will break an oath with thee.

Antonio.   I once did lend my body for his wealth;
Which, but for him that had your husband's ring,
Had quite miscarried: I dare be bound again,   270
My soul upon the forfeit, that your lord
Will never more break faith advisedly.

Portia.   Then you shall be his surety.   Give him this
And bid him keep it better than the other.

Antonio.   Here, Lord Bassanio; swear to keep this
        ring.

Bassanio.   By heaven, it is the same I gave the doctor!

Portia.   You are all amazed:
Here is a letter: read it at your leisure;
It comes from Padua, from Bellario: 280
There you shall find that Portia was the doctor,
Nerissa there her clerk: Lorenzo here
Shall witness I set forth as soon as you
And even but now return'd: I have not yet
Enter'd my house.   Antonio, you are welcome;
And I have better news in store for you
Than you expect: unseal this letter soon;
There you shall find three of your argosies
Are richly come to harbour suddenly:
You shall not know by what strange accident   290
I chanced on this letter.

Antonio.   I am dumb.

Bassanio.   Were you the doctor and I knew you not?

Gratiano.   Were you the clerk and yet I knew you
    not?

Antonio.   Sweet lady, you have given me life and
    living;
For here I read for certain that my ships
Are safely come to road.

Portia.   How now, Lorenzo!   300
My clerk hath some good comforts, too, for you.

Nerissa.   Ay, and I'll give them him without a fee.
There do I give to you and Jessica,
From the rich Jew, a special deed of gift,
After his death, of all he dies possess'd of.

Lorenzo.   Fair ladies, you drop manna in the way
Of starved people.

Portia.   It is almost morning,
And yet I am sure you are not satisfied
Of these events at full.   Let us go in;   310
And charge us there upon inter'gatories,
And we will answer all things faithfully.

Gratiano.   Well, while I live I'll fear no other thing
So sore as keeping safe Nerissa's ring.   [*Exeunt.*

NOTES

The first half of Scene I. is intended to give the audience some idea of the mood of the play as a whole, and at the same time to introduce them to Antonio, "The Merchant of Venice," and give them some necessary information as to his fortunes. In the sadness of Antonio the audience is given a suggestion of the ill-fortune which overtakes him in the course of the play; and in spite of his assurances that his "ventures" have nothing to do with his sadness, we cannot help feeling that the street-gossips, Salarino and Salanio, have in fact come very near the truth in their suggestion that "Antonio is sad to think upon his merchandise."

In the second half of the scene the audience makes the acquaintance of Bassanio, Lorenzo, and Gratiano; and in that part of the conversation in which Bassanio confides his plans to Antonio, we are given a charming picture of Portia, which prepares the audience for the scene which is to follow.

2. it. My sadness.

5. am to learn. Have yet to learn.

6. want-wit. Stupid fellow.

7. much ado. Much trouble.

to know myself. To recognize myself.

9. argosies. Large merchant vessels. The word *argosy* is derived from *Ragusa*, the name of a port on the Adriatic near Venice, which carried on a large trade with England.

portly. Puffed out by the wind.

10. signiors. Noblemen.

11. pageants. Antonio's vessels are compared to the gaily decorated barges or floats which formed part of the shows which were common, on the Thames or in the streets of London, in Shakespeare's day.

12. **overpeer.** Look down upon the little trading vessels.

13. **do them reverence.** Pay respect to them.

14. **they.** The large vessels of Antonio.

15. **venture.** Literally, something that is risked. Here, the vessels, exposed to danger.

16. I should be so concerned about my vessels that I could think of little else.

affections. Feelings.

17. **still.** Always.

18. To find out in what direction the wind was blowing, by holding up a blade of grass or by throwing some loose grass in the air.

19. **roads.** Roadsteads, where ships may ride safely at anchor.

22-3. If I should blow upon my broth to cool it I should be reminded of a wind at sea and that would make me shake with fear.

25. **the sandy hour-glass.** The hour-glass consists of two compartments, one of which is filled with sand. It takes an hour for the sand to run from the upper to the lower compartment. In Shakespeare's time, hour-glasses were placed in churches near the pulpit so that the minister might estimate the length of his sermon.

27. **Andrew.** Here, the name of a vessel.

docked in sand. Held fast in the sand.

28. **Vailing.** Lowering. The vessel is turned over on its side so that the top of the main-mast is lower than the sides (ribs).

29. **her burial.** The sand she is buried in.

32. **but.** Merely.

34. **Enrobe.** Clothe, cover.

35. **in a word.** To sum it all up.

worth. The vessel at one moment is worth so much, and the next moment worth nothing.

36-8. Can I think of this without at the same time thinking that if such a thing should happen to me it would make me sad?

42. **bottom.** Vessel.

43-4. I have not risked all my wealth upon what may happen this year.

52. **Janus.** A Roman deity, the god of gates and doors. He is represented as having two faces, the one grave, the other laughing. The word *January* is derived from "Janus."

54. **peep.** Why is this word appropriate?

55. **like parrots.** In a senseless fashion.

at a bag-piper. Related to "laugh," not to "parrots."

56. **other.** Others.

vinegar aspect. Sour expression of face.

58. **Nestor.** The oldest and gravest of the Greek heroes who fought at Troy.

64. **prevented.** Used here in the literal sense of "come in ahead of me," "anticipated me."

65. I have a high opinion of *your* worth!

67. **embrace the occasion.** Are glad of the opportunity.

69. **laugh.** Be merry together.

71. We see very little of you. Must you really go now?

72. We shall arrange to be at leisure when you are.

78. You have too much regard for worldly affairs.

79. **lose it.** Lose the enjoyment of it.

84. **old wrinkles.** This may mean either "the wrinkles of old age," or "plenty of wrinkles." *Old* is used very frequently by Shakespeare in this latter sense.

86. **mortifying.** Producing death. It was believed at one time that sighs and groans drained the blood from the heart.

88. **alabaster.** White marble. Over many of the tombs in Shakespeare's day there were placed marble images of those who were buried below. In a niche in the wall over Shakespeare's own grave in Trinity church, Stratford, there is an image of the poet "cut in alabaster."

89. **jaundice.** A disease which causes the skin to become yellow. It is sometimes brought on by violent emotion.

92-3.   The serious expression on the faces of these men is compared to the dull surface of the stagnant pond that is covered with scum.

cream and mantle.   Become coated with scum.

94-6.   They are determined to keep silent in order that they may gain a reputation (opinion) for wisdom, gravity and profound thoughtfulness (conceit).

97. **As who should say.**   As if some one should say.   *Who* is an indefinite pronoun.

Sir Oracle.   The word *oracle* is applied to any one who speaks words of great wisdom.   *Sir* in this case expresses contempt.

100-1.   "Even a fool when he holdeth his peace is counted wise; and he that shutteth his lips is esteemed a man of understanding." *Proverbs*, xxii., 28.

101. **when.**   Whereas.

102.   Supply *it* before *would*.

102-3.   If they should speak, those who heard them would be sure to call them fools, and thus come under the condemnation mentioned in Scripture.   See *Matthew*, v., 22.   "Whosoever shall say, Thou fool, shall be in danger of hell fire."

105-6.   Do not try to gain a reputation for wisdom by appearing melancholy.

gudgeon.   A fish that is easily caught, and not worth anything.

108. **exhortation.**   Sermon.   There is perhaps a humorous reference to the long sermons of the Puritan clergy.

112. **moe.**   More.   In older English *moe* was used with reference to number, while *more* was used with reference to quantity.

114. **for this gear.**   Either "for this occasion" or "as a result of this stuff that you have been speaking." *Gear* means, literally, material *prepared*; and it is commonly used in the sense of *stuff, matter, business, affair*.

116. **neat's tongue.**   Ox tongue.

117. **Is that any thing now?**   Is there any sense in what Gratiano has been saying?

127. **disabled mine estate.**   Weakened my resources.

128-9. Living in somewhat greater splendour than my scanty income would permit me to keep up.

something.   To some extent, somewhat; used adverbially.

130-1.   I am not complaining because I have to give up this extravagant style of living.

132. to come fairly off.   To free myself honourably.

133-4.   In which my life (time), which has been somewhat too extravagant, has left me involved.

134. gaged.   Pledged, involved.

136-7.   Knowing your love for me, I am warranted in confiding my plans and purposes to you.

140-1.   If it is something that may be looked upon as honourable.

143. occasions.   Necessities.

146. of the self-same flight.   Of the same weight and length, and feathered in the same way.

147. advisèd.   Careful.

149. childhood proof.   Experiment from my life as a child (Latin, *probare*, to test, to try).

150.   Because what I am about to say is just as innocent and free from deceit as my attempt in childhood to find the lost arrow.

153. self.   Selfsame.

155-6. or . . . or.   Either . . . or.

160.   In approaching the subject in this roundabout way, instead of appealing directly to my love.

To wind about.   As in the case of a hunter who approaches his game in a roundabout way so as to escape being seen.

circumstance.   Circumlocution.

162.   In doubting that I am willing to do my utmost to help you.

166. prest unto it.   Ready for it.   (Fr. *prêt*, ready).

167. Belmont.   An imaginary place.

richly left.   One who has had great riches left to her.

168-9.   To have wondrous virtues is better (fairer) than to be merely beautiful (fair).

169. **sometimes.** In former times.

172. Portia, the daughter of Cato the Roman patriot, was the wife of Marcus Brutus, who led the conspiracy against Caesar.

175-8. Colchos, or Colchis, was a country in Asia on the shores of the Black Sea. In the grove of Ares (Mars) in Colchis there was fastened to an oak tree a golden fleece, which was guarded by a dragon. This golden fleece was finally carried off by Jason, who sailed to Colchis, with a band of Greek heroes, in his famous ship the Argo. The story of Jason is told at length in Kingsley's *Greek Heroes*.

181. I have a mind *which* foretells (presages) me such success (thrift).

185. **commodity.** Merchandise.

188. **rack'd.** Stretched.

190. **presently.** Immediately.

191. **I no question make.** I have no doubt.

192. What is the difference between "of my trust" and "for my sake"?

Questions.

1. What do you learn about Antonio (*a*) from his conversation with Salarino and Salanio, and (*b*) from his conversation with Bassanio?

2. (*a*) What is it that leads Gratiano to make the long speech beginning, "Let me play the fool"?

(*b*) In what mood is he when he speaks it? What impression does this speech give you of his character?

3. (*a*) Bassanio confesses that he has lived in an extravagant style, and that he has wasted the money which he has already borrowed from Antonio. How is it then that with faults so great as these he is able to gain and hold the sympathy of the audience?

(*b*) "Bassanio is after all, a mere adventurer who is attracted to Portia because of her wealth."

Do you agree with this statement? Support your view by references to the text.

4. Compare the statement contained in lines 41-45 with that contained in lines 183-186. Can you reconcile these statements?

Scene II.

Following the description of Portia in Scene I., it is not difficult for us to picture the "room in Portia's house" in Belmont. The furnishings of the room itself are no doubt rich, but in keeping with the character of the owner. Portia we know is "fair" in the double sense of being both fair-haired and beautiful: Nerissa, as the name signifies, is dark, in contrast to her mistress. Portia, like Antonio, is sad, or rather "aweary of this great world"; and her weariness is plainly due to her anxiety as to the "choosing" of a husband. The conversation with Nerissa not only helps to bring out the characters of Portia and Nerissa, but gives us some insight into the circumstances of the "lottery"; and at the same time it prepares the way for a favourable reception of Bassanio, when the time at length comes for him to present himself as a suitor.

1. **By my troth.** Truly. **troth.** Truth.

7. **in the mean.** In a middle position, neither rich nor poor.

8-9. The man who has more money than he needs becomes gray-haired from the worry of looking after it; the man who has just sufficient for his needs has fewer anxieties and lives longer.

10. **sentences.** Maxims. When we say that a person is *sententious*, what do we mean?

13. **chapels.** A chapel is a smaller place of worship than a church.

17-20. The intellect, or reason, may lay down rules by which our bodily passions should be controlled; but when we are carried away by our passions we break the rules which we made for ourselves in our cooler moments. Our reason may be compared to an old cripple who sets a trap or net to catch a hare: and the passions of youth may be compared to the hare which jumps over the net.

20-1. This moralizing is not likely to help me in choosing a husband. **fashion.** Way.

23-4. Note the pun on *will*.

25. The double negative was common in Shakespeare's time.

28. **lottery.** Nerissa speaks of it as a lottery because the element of chance enters into it.

29. **chooses his meaning.** The choice of the caskets, as it appears later in the play, is a test of the characters of the different suitors.

36. **level at my affection.** Guess what my feelings are towards them.

38. **colt.** A wild, headstrong young fellow.

39-40. **appropriation to his own good parts.** Addition to his own good qualities.

41. **County Palatine.** Shakespeare uses *Count* and *County* with the same meaning. The word *Palatine* literally means "belonging to the palace." The County Palatine is then a Count who rules over lands connected with the king's palace.

43. **choose.** This may mean either, "Choose whomsoever you wish; I don't care," or "Choose your weapons, to fight me."

44-5. **the weeping philosopher.** Heraclitus of Ephesus, who lived about 513 B.C., was called the weeping philosopher because of his gloomy views of life.

47. **a death's head.** Skull and crossbones.

49. **by.** Regarding.

55. **every man in no man.** He has all the qualities of other men, but has no mind of his own.

throstle. Thrush.

55-6. **he falls straight a capering.** He begins straightway to dance.

59. **requite him.** Return his love.

60. Nerissa asks: "What is your opinion of Falconbridge?" Portia in her reply puns on the expression *say to*.

66. **a proper man's picture.** The picture of a handsome (proper) man.

67. **suited.** Dressed.

68. **doublet.** A close-fitting jacket, which was worn under the cloak.

round hose. Breeches, padded at the knees so that they were *round* in shape.

69. bonnet. Covering for the head.

72. charity. Friendliness.

73-4. Portia suggests that the Scottish lord is inferior in courage to the Englishman.

75. The figure is taken from a business transaction in which one man goes security for another. The French were the allies of the Scotch in their quarrels with the English.

sealed under. Signed his name and affixed his seal, as in the case of a legal document.

82. an the worst fall. If the worst happen.

89. contrary. Wrong.

97. sort. Way, method.

imposition. The conditions which he has imposed.

99. Sibylla. The word *sibyl* is a general term meaning prophetess. The reference here is to the Sibyl of Cumae (in southern Italy). She is said to have obtained from Apollo the promise that the years of her life should be as many in number as the grains of sand she was able to hold in her hand.

100. Diana. The virgin goddess, who was regarded as the symbol of chastity.

107. Montferrat. Near Genoa.

116. four. This is an error. There were six in all.

122. condition of a saint. Goodness, saintly disposition.

123. complexion of a devil. Black skin.

123-4. I should prefer to have him for my father-confessor than for my husband.

125. Sirrah. A form of address used towards inferiors.

126. Whiles. While. *Whiles* is the old genitive case form, with an adverbial value.

QUESTIONS.

1. (*a*) In the conversation between Nerissa and Portia what information is given as to the character of the "lottery" by which Portia is to be won?

(*b*) How does Portia regard this lottery?

2. (a) We are told before the close of the scene that the suitors whom Nerissa names have decided to return to their homes. What reason is given for their decision?

(b) What is the dramatist's purpose in introducing a detailed description of these suitors into this scene?

3. (a) In the reference to Bassanio (ll. 105-114), what further information is given regarding his character?

(b) What has Bassanio already said (in Scene I.) regarding his former visit to Portia?

(c) Why is the reference to Bassanio introduced into this scene?

Scene III.

Under ordinary circumstances the plan of Antonio to borrow money on his credit should have been carried out without difficulty. But, unfortunately, Bassanio, who evidently knew nothing of Antonio's relations to the money-lenders on the Rialto, goes to the one man with whom Antonio is on terms of bitter enmity. The enmity of Antonio and Shylock is due partly to the hatred which existed between Jew and Christian, but chiefly to the fact that Antonio does not believe in taking interest on loans,—especially when money is lent to a friend,—and that he has shown his hatred towards Shylock openly on the Rialto. Shylock sees in the request of Bassanio an opportunity to revenge himself on his enemy; but the idea of taking interest in the form of a pound of flesh evidently does not at once occur to him. It is only when he is driven to justify the taking of interest by reference to the example of Jacob that he conceives the idea of the bond. At first sight it might appear unreasonable that a bond such as this should ever have been proposed, and that when proposed it should have been accepted by Antonio. But in the course of the conversation regarding the conduct of Jacob, Antonio had said in effect:—"Interest in the form of flesh and blood in the case of sheep and goats, where there is a natural increase, may perhaps be justified; but the taking of interest on money, which is barren, is a different thing; and, besides, one should not take interest from a friend." "But," replies Shylock, "I wish to be friends with you and to buy your favour by doing you this kindness; and just because you agree that interest in the case of flesh and blood is all right, let us say in this case, merely as a piece of merry sport, that the interest will be a pound of your flesh." Bassanio is shrewd enough to suspect the motives of Shylock, but Antonio is confident of the return of his vessels, and he is, at the same time, too proud, perhaps, to show any secret misgivings that he may have before either his friend Bassanio or the Jew; and so, in spite of the protests of Bassanio, he consents to put his seal to the bond.

1. ducat. A coin worth between four and five shillings of Elizabethan money. Three thousand ducats would be the equivalent of about $25,000 in modern currency. A *ducat* is, literally, a coin issued by a *duchy*.

4. the which. In Elizabethan English *the* was frequently used before *which* to make the pronoun more definite.

5. bound. As a surety.

7. May you. Are you able?

stead me. Be of use to me; assist me.

pleasure me. Do me this favour?

12. good. Financially sound.

17. in supposition. Doubtful. It is not certain that his ships will return safely: we can only suppose that they will.

18. Tripolis. A port in Syria which carried on an extensive trade with Venice; not to be confused with Tripoli in north Africa.

the Indies. The West Indies.

19. the Rialto. The Exchange of Venice was situated upon the island known as *Rialto* (Ital. *riva alta*, high bank). The name Rialto is also applied to a bridge over the Grand Canal, built in 1588-91; but the reference in this case is to the Exchange, not to the bridge.

21. squandered. Scattered.

28. assured. Shylock uses the word in a stronger sense than Bassanio.

29. bethink me. Think it over.

31-2. See *Matthew*, viii., 28-32.

32. **Nazarite.** In the translations of the Bible previous to the authorized version of 1611, "Nazarite" is always used in place of "Nazarene."

conjured. *Conjure* (pr. *kun'-jer*) means "to influence by magic": *conjure* (pr. *kon-ju'r*) means "to call upon by oath." In which sense is the word here used?

36. Supply *that* before *comes*.

37. **Signior,** or signor, is the English form of the Italian *Signore*, which is equivalent of *Sir* or *Mr*.

38. **publican.** The Roman tax-gatherer, who was bitterly hated by the Jews.

fawning. Courting favour by cringing. The Roman publican was more likely to be insolent than fawning, in his treatment of the Jews. But possibly Shakespeare is thinking of the abject humility of the publican in the New Testament parable (*Luke*, xviii., 10-14).

40. **for that.** Because.

low simplicity. Contemptible foolishness.

41. **gratis.** Free of charge.

42. **usance.** Interest.

43. If I can get an advantage over him. The metaphor is taken from wrestling.

44. **feed fat.** Satisfy to the full.

46. **there.** On the Rialto.

47. **thrift.** Profits.

57. **Rest you fair.** *Rest* is used in the sense of *keep*, and the expression means, "God keep you fortunate."

60. **excess.** Interest: the amount paid in excess of the principal.

61. **ripe.** Pressing.

62. **possess'd.** Informed.

68. **Methought.** It seemed to me.

69. **Upon advantage.** By taking or giving interest.

70. It is not my custom.

71-80. See *Genesis*, xxvii.-xxx.

78. **were compromised.** Had come to an agreement.

79. eanlings. New-born lambs.

pied. Spotted.

86. Was this story inserted in the Bible in order to justify the taking of interest?

89. note me. Listen to what I have to say. Antonio, however, does not listen, but turns to talk to Bassanio.

91. See *Matthew*, iv., 4-6.

92. producing holy witness. Quoting Scripture as evidence.

98. beholding. Beholden, obliged.

101. usances. Interest.

102. Still. Always.

103. sufferance. Endurance.

badge. Distinguishing mark. In Venice the outward badge of the Jew was a yellow cap, which in accordance with Venetian law he was compelled to wear.

105. gaberdine. Cloak.

108. Go to. Away with you!

110. void your rheum. Spit.

111. foot me. Kick me out of the way.

116. in a bondman's key. In the tone of voice which a slave might use.

117. With bated breath. Scarcely breathing; *bated* means "lessened."

127. breed. Increase. It might be all right, Antonio argues, to take the "breed" or natural increase of sheep or goats, but metal is "barren" and does not increase.

129-30. Reconstruct the clause so as to make it grammatically correct.

face. Appearance of justice.

134. doit. A Dutch coin worth less than half a farthing.

143. the condition. The conditions of the contract.

144. nominated for. Stated as.

equal. Exact.

150. dwell. Remain.

153. return. When his ships come back.

156.   Supply *to* before *suspect*.

158.   **break his day.**   Fail to meet his payments at the time appointed.

161.   **estimable.**   Valuable.

162.   **muttons, beefs.**   In Shakespeare's time the words "mutton" and "beef" were sometimes applied to the living animals, where we should now say "sheep" and "ox."

164.   **so.**   Well and good.

165.   **wrong me not.**   Do not be so unjust as to suspect me.

170.   Left in charge of a careless fellow (unthrifty knave) whom I am afraid (fearful) to trust.

171.   **presently.**   Immediately.

173.   **Hie thee.**   Hasten.

QUESTIONS.

1. In his speech beginning, "How like a fawning publican he looks!" Shylock gives three reasons for his hatred of Antonio. What are these reasons?

2. "At the beginning of the scene Shylock apparently has in mind no definite plan of revenge. The idea of the bond in which the forfeit should be a pound of flesh, is evidently the outcome of his conversation with Bassanio and Antonio." What evidence do you find in the scene to justify this point of view?

3. (*a*) Point out any details in the scene which throw light upon (i) Antonio's treatment of Shylock in the past, and (ii) his feelings towards Shylock in the present scene.

(*b*) Do you consider that the conduct of Antonio in this scene is in any way open to criticism?

4. Under ordinary circumstances it would seem a most unnatural thing that any man should propose to take interest in the form of a pound of flesh. By what means has Shakespeare contrived to make this appear to be a very natural proposal?

5. In view of the fact that Shylock apparently has good reasons for wishing to disarm the suspicions of Antonio and Bassanio, how do you account for his outburst of passion in lines 99-122?

SUMMARY OF ACT I.

In Act I. the audience is introduced to the four leading characters in the play,—Antonio, Bassanio, Shylock, and Portia. In the sadness of Antonio, in the beginning of Scene I., there is a vague hint of approaching misfortune, which gives to the audience a suggestion as to the mood of the play as a whole. In the first two scenes of the play the foundations of the casket story are laid. In the conversation between Portia and Nerissa we are given an insight into the character of the "lottery" by which Portia is to be chosen; and at the very outset our sympathies are enlisted on the side of Bassanio. Out of the casket story there grows the story of the pound of flesh; for it is because of the "ripe wants" of Bassanio that Antonio is led to sign the bond in borrowing money from Shylock. Act I. thus serves as an introduction to the play as a whole, inasmuch as it introduces us to the main characters in the play, and gives us an insight into the plans of Bassanio and of Shylock, out of which the two main stories in the play are developed.

ACT II.—SCENE I.

In Scene I. we are given an opportunity to judge of the character of Morocco,—the first of the suitors who makes a choice of the caskets. But before making any study of his character it is worth while for us to try to picture the scene itself,—the room in Portia's house, Portia and her train, the Moorish prince and his followers. The stage direction of the first folio describes Morocco as a "tawnie Moor, all in white," and we can imagine what a striking contrast the Moorish prince and his train, with dark faces set off with white turbans, would form to Portia and her retinue. The magnificence of Morocco's followers is no doubt in keeping with the fine bearing and handsome figure of the prince. In spite of his vanity and love of display, we are pleased with the gallantry of Morocco, and notwithstanding his boastfulness, there is something in the boyish frankness of his manner that attracts us. For obvious reasons we do not wish him to marry Portia, but strangely enough we have little anxiety as to the outcome of his choice.

1. **Mislike.**   Dislike.

2. **livery.** Dress, garb; the uniform worn by a servant to show to what house he belonged. Morocco explains that his dark complexion is merely the dress which his master the sun has given him to wear.

burnished. Glowing.

3. **near bred.** Near which I have been brought up.

4. **fairest.** Of the lightest complexion.

5. **Phœbus.** The sun-god.

6. **make incision.** Cut into the veins to draw blood.

7. **reddest.** Red blood was considered a sign of courage.

8. **aspect.** Countenance, outward appearance.

9. **fear'd.** Frightened, terrified.

10. **best-regarded.** Those held in greatest esteem.

clime. Country.

13-4. Portia explains that in making a choice she is not wholly influenced by any fine distinctions as to the outward appearance of her suitors. Her eyes, if she depended upon them, would no doubt give her critical (nice) directions as to which one she should choose.

15-6. Besides, she adds, I am not permitted to choose of my own free will: my destiny is to be decided by lottery.

17. **scanted.** Restricted, limited.

18. **hedged.** Set a limit to my actions.

wit. Here, wisdom, judgment.

19. **His wife who.** The wife of him who.

20. **stood as fair.** Would have stood as good a chance. Past subjunctive.

21. Note the touch of humour here. Who are the different suitors to whom she refers?

23. **Even for that.** To the vain Morocco, Portia's answer was not so flattering as he might have wished.

25. **scimitar.** A short curved sword.

26. **the Sophy,** or Sufi. The Shah of Persia.

27. **That.**   The antecedent is "Prince," not "scimitar."

fields.   Battles.

Sultan Solyman.   Solyman the Magnificent, Sultan of Turkey (1490-1566), who was defeated by the Persians in 1535.

32. **alas the while!**   An expression of regret that times have changed.   Compare, "Woe the while!"   "Woe the day!"

33. **Hercules and Lichas.**   Hercules was a hero of Greek mythology, famous for his great strength.   Lichas was his attendant, or page.

33-9.   If they play at dice to decide which is the stronger, Lichas may win, although he is in reality so much weaker than Hercules.   So also, argues Morocco, the choosing of the right casket is all a matter of chance, and although I am so much better than all the other suitors, I may nevertheless lose.

36. **Alcides.**   Hercules was also called Alcides, because of the fact that the name of his grandfather was Alcæus.

44. **be advised.**   Take heed what you do.

45. **Nor will not.**   Neither will I speak to lady afterward. The double negative is used for the sake of emphasis.

47. **temple.**   The church or chapel where the oath must be taken.

50. **blest.**   Most blest.

QUESTIONS.

1. (a) By what means does Morocco attempt to win the admiration of Portia?

(b) "His boastfulness is rendered less disagreeable because of his show of gallantry towards Portia."   Explain.

(c) "Morocco evidently considered that the choice of the right casket was purely a matter of chance, rather than a test of character."   Justify this statement by reference to the text.

2. In lines 40-44 Portia states one of the most important conditions of the "lottery."   What was the object of Portia's father in imposing this condition?

Scene II.

This scene affords relaxation and amusement for the audience. The entertainment which Launcelot provides is, however, not of a high order intellectually. He does not possess the ready wit of the professional jester, but his fun consists chiefly in absurdities of speech and in good-natured buffoonery which is brought out in the acting of the play.

During the course of the scene we are given some hint of the preparations which Bassanio is making to prosecute his suit with Portia, and we learn at the same time that he is planning that very evening to give a feast to his "best-esteemed acquaintance" before he sets out for Belmont.

8. with thy heels. To scorn anything with the heels is to kick up the heels at it in contempt. Launcelot no doubt intends "with thy heels" to be taken with "running."

9. pack. Be off.

'Via!' Away with you.

15-6. His father, he means to say, was not quite honest. In speaking of his dishonesty Launcelot compares it to the unpleasant taste of milk which has become burned in the bottom of the pan.

15. did something smack. Had a somewhat unpleasant taste.

grow to. Literally, stuck to the bottom of the pot or pan.

21. God bless the mark. If I may be pardoned for saying so. The expression is said to have originated in the habit of "blessing" birthmarks in new-born infants. A birthmark was supposed to be due to the influence of evil spirits, and the blessing, with the sign of the cross, was intended to counteract this evil influence.

23. saving your reverence. This is used with practically the same meaning as "God bless the mark" in line 21.

24. incarnal. Some texts have "incarnation." Launcelot of course means *incarnate*, *i.e.*, in the flesh.

32. sand-blind. This word is a corruption of *sam-blind*, that is, "semi blind." Launcelot uses the word *sand* in its ordinary meaning.

high. Quite.

33. confusions. Conclusions.

38. marry. Mary; a mild form of oath.

40. sonties. This may be a corruption of either (1) *saints*, or (2) *sanctities*.

44. raise the waters. Raise a storm; or, perhaps, bring tears to his eyes.

48. well to live. Either, in good health, or, a good-living man.

49. a'. He.

52. ergo. Therefore. This is a Latin word which Launcelot has picked up, and which he uses in order to show off before Old Gobbo.

54. an't. If it.

56. father. The word "father" was commonly used in addressing an old man, and Old Gobbo evidently takes it in this sense.

57-8. Launcelot uses these high-sounding phrases which he has heard at the play-houses, without much idea of what they mean.

the sisters three. The three Fates, in Greek mythology.

63. hovel-post. A post holding up the roof of a hovel or shed.

87. Lord worshipped might he be! Merely an exclamation of surprise. Launcelot has knelt down with the back of his head towards his father, who mistakes his long hair for a beard.

89. fill-horse. Shaft-horse. "Fill" is another form of the word "thill," a shaft.

97. set up my rest. Determined. The origin of the expression is uncertain. It is possible that the phrase was originally used in gaming, where "to set up one's rest" meant "to stake everything."

100. tell. Count.

101. me. To please me.

103. liveries. Uniforms.

110. anon. By and by.

113. Gramercy! Many thanks (Fr. *grand merci*).

116. specify. Certify.

117. infection. Affection, desire

122. **cater-cousins.** Close friends. The origin of the expression is doubtful. Perhaps it was originally applied to people who were on sufficiently intimate terms to "cater" to one another.

125. **frutify.** Certify.

126. **a dish of doves.**   Doves were a common article of food in Italy.

128. **impertinent.** Launcelot of course means *pertinent*.

134. **defect.** Effect, issue.

138. **preferr'd.** Recommended.

preferment. Promotion.

141. **The old proverb.** "The grace of God is gear enough."

parted. Shared.

147. **guarded.** With more braid or facings. The braid with which a garment was trimmed was said to "guard" or protect the edges of the cloth. Bassanio's purpose in making Launcelot's livery more guarded was no doubt to mark him out as a jester.

148.   Launcelot of course means the opposite of what he says.

150. **a fairer table.** Better fortune. The "table" is the palm of the hand from which one's fortune is told.

which doth offer, etc. Two interpretations are possible. *Which* may refer to *man*, in which case there is a reference to the old custom of holding up the hand in taking an oath,— with the result that the man's "table" would be displayed. On the other hand, *which* may refer to *table*, and in this case the meaning must be that the "table" is to be trusted, as upon oath, that he shall have good fortune.

151. **Go to.** Away with you. Launcelot is addressing an imaginary person.

simple. Used ironically here and in the remainder of the speech.

157. **for this gear.** See the note on Act I, Scene I, l. 114.

163. **acquaintance.** This is plural.

hie thee. Hasten.

175. **Parts.** Qualities.

178. **Something too liberal.** Somewhat too free.

184. **sober habit.** Serious manner.

186. **demurely.** Soberly.

189. **Use all the observance of civility.** Pay attention to all the requirements of good breeding.

190. Like one who has made a study of looking serious in order to please his grandmother.

Questions

1. (*a*) Point out the expressions in this scene which are likely to prejudice the audience still further against Shylock.

(*b*) What is it that attracts Launcelot to the service of Bassanio?

(*c*) How does Bassanio regard Launcelot?

2. Old Gobbo does not appear elsewhere in the play. What then is the purpose of introducing him in this scene?

Scene III

Under ordinary circumstances an audience would naturally be prejudiced against the daughter of Shylock. But Shakespeare has represented her as beautiful and has besides made it clear to us that though she is a daughter to his blood she is not to his manners. As a matter of fact, Shylock appears to us all the more miserly and mean when his home is such that his own daughter is moved to say, "Our house is hell." But here the dramatist is on delicate ground, for no matter how miserly Shylock may have been, the audience has a deep-rooted feeling that Jessica should be loyal to her father. The dramatist however disarms our criticism by showing that Jessica did in reality possess these filial feelings, and that her duty towards her father is at "strife" with her love for Lorenzo.

3. **some taste of tediousness.** A little of its dreariness.

10. **exhibit.** Prohibit, or inhibit; prevent, restrain.

11. **adieu.** Note the pun.

17. **manners.** His disposition which shows itself in his way of living.

18. **strife.** Her love for Lorenzo in conflict with her duty towards her father.

QUESTIONS.

1. Point out the details of this scene that are intended to give the audience a favourable impression of Jessica.

2. What interpretation does the dramatist intend us to put upon the speech of Launcelot?

SCENE IV.

This scene prepares the way for the elopement of Lorenzo and Jessica. Lorenzo has proposed that in the midst of the feast which Bassanio is giving to his friends, they "slink away" unperceived, put on their masks, and return to the banquet in disguise. At first Lorenzo's companions raise objections, but just at this moment Launcelot comes in with a letter from Jessica. Gratiano at once guesses Lorenzo's secret; and now that they see the reasons for Lorenzo's proposal, the three friends are quite eager to go forward with the masque. In Lorenzo's speech at the close of the scene we get another glimpse into the character of Jessica. It is she, and not the dreamy Lorenzo, who has planned all the details of the elopement, and has directed how he shall take her from her father's house.

1. **Nay.** Lorenzo's companions have evidently been raising objections.

5. We have not yet engaged torch-bearers for ourselves.

6. It will be a poor affair unless we arrange it with some taste and skill.

quaintly. Prettily, gracefully, artistically. In modern English the word *quaint* has come to have the meaning of *odd*, *old-fashioned*.

12. **break up.** Break open the seal.

12-3. Jessica had told Launcelot to deliver the letter "secretly." Does he do so?

22. **this.** Probably some money.

25. **masque.** A masquerade in which the actors wore masques and carried torches.

38. **gentle.**   Possibly a pun on the word *Gentile*.

39.   May misfortune never dare to cross her path.

40. **she.**   Misfortune.

41. **faithless.**   Unbelieving.

QUESTIONS.

1. How do you account for the fact that Gratiano, Salarino, and Salanio change their minds so suddenly regarding the masque?

2. "What Launcelot *does* is more expressive than what he *says*, in this scene."   Explain.

3. Point out any details in this scene that are intended to prepare the audience for the two following scenes.

SCENE V.

In Scene V. the audience is given a further glimpse into Shylock's home life and an insight into his relations towards his daughter Jessica.   In his reference to Launcelot we see something of his miserly disposition; and the mean suspicion with which he regards his own daughter forms some justification for her conduct towards him.

1. Emphasize *see*.

4. **What, Jessica!**   Shylock calls Jessica.   *What* and *why* (l. 7), are exclamations intended to attract her attention.

gormandize.   Eat like a glutton.

13. **bid forth.**   Invited out.

19. **a-brewing.**   The prefix *a* is derived from the preposition *on* which governed the gerund *brewing*.

towards my rest.   To prevent me from being at ease.

20. **to-night.**   Last night.

22. **reproach.**   Launcelot means *approach*; but Shylock prefers to take the word *reproach* literally.

26-9. There is, of course, no sense in what Launcelot says.

27. **Black Monday.**   On Easter Monday in the year 1360 the army of Edward III. was besieging Paris, and the day was

so bitterly cold that many men died on horseback. Easter Monday was thereafter very commonly spoken of as Black Monday.

28. Ash Wednesday. The first day of Lent.

32. wry-neck'd fife. The old English fife had a curved mouth-piece and hence may be described as "wry-neck'd"; but perhaps the dramatist has in mind the fact that the fifer is "wry-necked" while he is playing it.

33. casements. Windows opening on hinges.

35. varnish'd. Painted or, perhaps, covered with a masque.

38. Jacob's staff. A reference to *Genesis*, xxxii., 10, where Jacob says, "For with my staff I passed over this Jordan."

45. Who will be worth your looking at. There is a play upon the expression, "Worth a Jew's eye,"—that is, worth a great deal of money. In the days when it was a common practice to extort money from wealthy Jews by threats of torture, the unfortunate victim was sometimes forced to pay large sums on the penalty of losing an eye if he failed to pay.

46. The Israelites were the descendants of Isaac the son of Abraham by his wife Sarah. The Ishmaelites were the descendants of Ishmael, the son of Abraham by Hagar, his bondwoman. After the birth of Isaac, Sarah, who was jealous of Hagar, persuaded Abraham to send Hagar and her son Ishmael away. The Jew, therefore, looked upon the descendants of Hagar as outcasts, and Shylock uses the term "fool of Hagar's offspring" as equivocal to, "Gentile fool."

48. patch. Fool, clown. The professional jester wore a motley coat, which looked as if it were made of "patches" of different colours.

49. profit. Profitable work.

50. drones. Drones are the male bees, which do no work and are cast out of the hive by the worker-bees at the end of the season.

56. If you close the house firmly or tightly (fast), you will find it fast closed upon your return.

58. crost. thwarted, interfered with.

QUESTIONS.

1. (*a*) Shylock says to Launcelot, "Thou shalt not gormandize, as thou hast done with me." What has Launcelot already said (Act II., Sc. II.) as to the fare in Shylock's home?

(*b*) What reason does Shylock give for "parting with" Launcelot?

2. (*a*) "I am bid forth to supper, Jessica." On what two occasions has Shylock's invitation to supper already been mentioned in the play?

(*b*) What reason does Shylock give for accepting?

3. (*a*) What do you gather from this scene regarding Shylock's feelings towards Jessica?

(*b*) Do you find anything to criticise in Jessica's conduct towards her father?

(*c*) Why did Shylock say, "Perhaps I will return immediately"?

4. "At several points in the scene Shylock sets out, but after he has gone a few steps he returns." In what parts of the scene should the actor, in your opinion, represent Shylock as setting forth?

SCENE VI.

In order to add interest to the elopement of Jessica, the dramatist has made use of a number of special devices in this present scene. The comments of Salarino and Gratiano as they wait for the tardy Lorenzo in front of Shylock's house, are especially suited to a love scene. The masquerade too adds an element of picturesqueness to the elopement; and the fact that Jessica assumes the disguise of a boy gives the excuse for an exchange of banter, in which we see another side of her character. An elopement is sometimes rendered exciting because there is a certain amount of danger in it; but in this case it is the theft of jewels and ducats that help to supply the romantic element. The actual masquerade is, to be sure, never carried out, but the preparations that have been made for it have served their purpose; and the scene closes with a reference to the love affair of Bassanio, in which more important issues are at stake.

1. **pent-house.** Literally, a lean-to, a shed. Here, probably a house with a sloping roof projecting over the street. *Penthouse* is a corruption of the word *pentice*, (O. F. *apentis*, a shed).

4-5. It is strange that he is late, for lovers are always ahead of time.

6. **Venus' pigeons.** The doves which drew the chariot of Venus, the goddess of love.

6-8. Salarino is explaining how it is that "lovers ever run before the clock." Newly betrothed lovers, he says in effect, are much more eager to keep their engagements, and so confirm their betrothal, than they are to keep other engagements to which they have pledged their word.

7. **To seal love's bonds.** To make sure of their betrothal, just as one puts his seal to a legal document (bond) to make it binding.

8. **obliged faith.** He is probably thinking here of people who are married as compared with those who are merely betrothed.

9. **That ever holds.** That is true in all cases.

11-12. No horse ever comes back from a journey with the same spirit with which he set out. Shakespeare may perhaps have been thinking of the manoeuvres which in former times horses were put through at tournaments or at the circus.

11. **untread.** Retrace.

12. **His tedious measures.** His paces which have now become wearisome.

unbated. Undiminished.

13. **that are.** That exist.

15. **younker.** Young man, youth (Dutch *jong*, young, and *heer*, gentleman).

16. **scarfed.** Either decked with flags, or fitted out freshly with sails.

17. **wanton.** Playful, sportive.

19. **over-weather'd ribs.** The sides worn by the wind and waves.

23. **abode.** Delay.

28. **for more certainty.** In order that I may be more certain.

29. **Albeit.** Although.

38. **exchange.** Change of dress.

45. **good sooth.** In truth.

light. Giddy, foolish.

46. The duty (office) of the torch-bearer is to show (discover) the way.

49. **garnish.** Dress.

51. **the close night.** The darkness which conceals us and keeps our secrets.

53. **gild.** Here, supply myself with gold.

55. **hood.** The hood was no doubt part of Gratiano's disguise.

a Gentile. A pun on the word *gentle*, meaning "well-born."

56. **Beshrew me.** Plague upon me; a mild form of oath.

but I love her. If I do not love her.

61. **constant.** Faithful, steadfast.

66. **Fie, fie.** Shame upon you for delaying so long.

68. **come about.** Veered, taken a favourable change.

69. **presently.** At once.

71. **on't.** Of it.

QUESTIONS.

1. In Scene IV., line 8, Lorenzo says, "Tis now but four o'clock." By reference to Scenes II., IV. and VI., show (*a*) at what hour the supper was to be held, (*b*) at what hour the masque was to take place, (*c*) where Lorenzo and his friends were to meet at supper time, and (*d*) where they were to meet when ready for the masque.

2. (*a*) On what other occasion in the play does Gratiano indulge in moralizing?

(*b*) Is there anything in the first part of this scene that would lead you to think that Gratiano's speech (ll. 9-20) is spoken in a playful rather than a serious mood?

3. (*a*) What means does the dramatist use in this scene to give the audience a favourable impression of Jessica?

(*b*) "Instead of condemning Jessica for robbing her father of gold and jewels, the audience are ready to approve of her action." How do you account for this?

SCENE VII.

In a previous scene we were introduced to the Prince of
Morocco and had an opportunity to form an estimate of his
character. In this scene his character is put to the test, and
we are interested in seeing whether or not our former estimate
was a just one. For a more detailed study of Morocco as he
appears in these two scenes, see page xviii of the Introduction.

1. **discover.** Reveal.

2. **several.** Different.

8. **all as blunt.** Quite as harsh as the lead is dull.

12. **withal.** As well, in addition.

13. May some god direct me to judge rightly. *Direct* is
subjunctive expressing a wish.

20. **golden.** Noble.

dross. The impurities which are drained off when metal is
being refined.

22. **virgin hue.** Clear white colour, suggesting purity.

25. **even.** Impartial.

26. **rated by thy estimation.** Judged by your real value
(Lat. *æstimo*, I value); or perhaps, judged by the opinion in
which others hold you.

30. **disabling.** Disparagement, underrating.

36. **graved.** Engraved, cut.

40. **shrine.** A sacred place, usually a church, which is
hallowed by its association with some saint. The reference
here is, no doubt, to the image of the saint within the shrine.

this mortal breathing saint. The images of the saints in the
shrines were made of marble; but Portia is a living human
(mortal) saint.

41. **Hyrcanian deserts.** Hyrcania was a district in Persia,
south-east of the Caspian sea.

vasty. Desolate.

42. **throughfares.** Thoroughfares.

44-5. The spray is thrown so high that it seems as if the
ocean were trying to reach the clouds.

49. **like.** Likely.

50-1. It would be too coarse a metal to form a coffin to incloco hcr shroud in the grave where it could not be seen.

cerecloth. Cloth dipped in melted wax, in which it was customary to wrap the dead body.

52. **immured.** Inclosed; literally, walled in.

53. At the period when the play was written, gold was worth ten times as much as silver.

56. **an angel.** The coin known as an angel was worth about ten shillings. Upon one side it bore the image of the arch-angel Michael slaying the dragon.

57. **insculp'd upon.** Bears the image engraved on the outside.

60. **thrive I as I may.** Let the result be whatsoever it will.

65. **A carrion Death.** A skull. The word *carrion* is ordinarily used in speaking of putrefying flesh. In this case Morocco uses it merely to express his feelings of disgust.

74. **inscroll'd.** Written in this scroll. If he had chosen wisely, he would, instead, have found Portia's picture in the casket.

75. **cold.** Dead, ended.

80. **A gentle riddance.** We are glad to get rid of him so easily.

81. **complexion.** Used here with a double meaning, referring to the colour of his skin and to his disposition.

QUESTIONS.

1. In what respect is Morocco's reasoning, in lines 15-20 at fault?

2. To what extent did Morocco's gallantry influence his judgment in his choice of the caskets?

3. How does the expression, "Why, that's the lady," in line 31 differ in meaning from the same expression in line 38? Show this difference of meaning by your reading.

4. Express the ideas contained in the inscription (ll. 67-75) in your own language.

Scene VIII.

In this scene we see the effect of the elopement upon Shylock. When he discovers his loss he at once jumps to the conclusion that Bassanio, the friend of Lorenzo, had something to do with the elopement and the loss of his ducats and jewels; and it is a natural thing to suppose that he will attempt to revenge himself upon Antonio when the occasion offers. Ominously enough, just at this juncture a hint is thrown out that one of Antonio's richest vessels has been lost; and as if to arouse our sympathy for Antonio, the scene concludes with an account of his unselfish affection for his friend Bassanio.

4. raised. Aroused.

9. gondola. A Venetian boat.

13. passion. An outburst of emotion.

28. well-remember'd. I am glad you thought of that. It reminds me of something I wanted to tell you.

29. reason'd. Talked.

30. the narrow seas. The English Channel.

32. fraught. Laden.

35. You were best. It would be (were) best for you.

41. Slubber. To do a thing carelessly; hence, to spoil by being in too great a hurry.

44. mind of love. Loving mind.

46. ostents. Shows, outward appearances.

47. conveniently. Suitably.

50. affection. Feelings.

sensible. Sensitive.

54. quicken. Enliven, cheer.

embraced heaviness. His sadness to which he seems to cling.

Questions.

1. Judging by his outcries (ll. 16-23) what are the real reasons for Shylock's passion?

2. Why is it that Shylock is likely to try to revenge himself on Antonio (ll. 26-27) for his daughter's flight?

3. What is the dramatist's purpose in mentioning the Venetian vessel that has miscarried in the English Channel (29-32)?

Scene IX.

The greater part of this scene is devoted to the choice of the caskets by Arragon; and a detailed study of his character as revealed in the scene will be found in the Introduction, page xviii. Arragon has no sooner taken his departure than a servant enters with news of the arrival of a messenger from Bassanio. The "young Venetian" who is the forerunner of Bassanio has evidently created a favourable impression, if we are to judge by the air of importance with which the servant of Portia announces his arrival.

4. his election. His choice of the caskets.

7. Straight. Straightway, at once.

21. address'd me. Prepared myself to choose.

21-2. Fortune now to my heart's hope. May fortune give me what I most desire.

27-8. meant by. Meant for.

20. fond. Foolish.

30. martlet. The martin, which builds under the eaves of houses and barns.

32. In the place where it is exposed to the full force of accidents (casualty).

34. jump. Agree.

35. barbarous multitudes. The crowd of common people who are rude in manner.

39. go about. Make the effort.

40. cozen. Cheat.

39-41. Arragon says in effect, "A man who is lacking in merit cannot succeed (cozen fortune) except by dishonourable means.

43. estates. Social position. As used here the word has no reference to property.

degrees. Distinctions in rank.

46. cover. Put on their hats, in the presence of those whom they have found to be unworthy of their respect.

48-51. How many men of humble birth would be deprived of their high rank, which rightfully belongs to the nobility; and how many men of noble birth who have lost their rank and fortune, would be restored to their rightful place. There is a confusion of figures here. *Gleaned, seed,* and *chaff* refer to the separation of wheat from chaff; while *new-varnished* suggests the brightening up of something that has been allowed to become dull from neglect.

53. assume desert. Assume that I am deserving.

55. Too long a pause. You have wasted your time in deliberating.

56. blinking. The eyes are weak and lacking in intelligence.

57. schedule. Written paper, scroll.

63-4. Arragon has shown poor judgment in choosing and now he finds fault with the result. Portia reminds him that he who makes mistakes (offends) is, by the very nature of things, unfitted to be a judge.

offices. Duties, functions.

69. shadows. In the case of Arragon, the shadow which he worshipped was his own "merit" or deserving.

71. I wis is derived from the old English adverb *iwis* meaning "certainly." Owing to its resemblance to the expression *I wist*, meaning "I knew," the notion arose that the *i* of *iwis* was a pronoun and that *wis* was a present tense form of the verb *wist.* As here used, the expression may mean either *certainly*, or *I know.*

75. you are sped. You are done with; your fate is decided.

81. wroth. Here, misery, disappointment.

84. wit. Cleverness. Portia is sarcastic.

85. heresy. False doctrine.

89. what would my lord? What do you wish, my lord? Portia is making fun of the pompous manner of her servant.

93. sensible regreets. Substantial greetings in the form of rich gifts.

sensible. Such as appeal to the senses.

94. To wit. Namely.

commends and courteous breath. Salutations and courteous words.

95. **Yet.** Thus far, up to this time.

96. **likely.** Promising.

98. **costly.** Rich, splendid.

102. **high-day.** Holiday; hence, unusual, making a special display.

104. **post.** Speedy messenger.

105. O Love, if it be thy will, may it be Bassanio who has come.

QUESTIONS.

1. Which of the conditions mentioned by Portia and Arragon in ll. 5-18 have already been stated earlier in the play? Give definite references.

2. In what way does Portia show her dislike of Arragon in this scene?

3. Portia says, in referring to Arragon, "O these deliberate fools!" Justify the use of the word *deliberate* as applied to Arragon.

4. Arragon condemns people who choose by show, and he argues that honour should in all cases be "purchased by the merit of the wearer." What is there, then, in his speech to which the audience can take exception?

5. The arrival of Arragon had not been previously announced in the play. What purpose, then, is served by the announcement of the approach of Bassanio?

SUMMARY OF ACT II.

In Act II. two different suitors, Morocco and Arragon, make their choice of the caskets. Morocco chooses the golden casket partly because of its showy exterior and partly because the inscription appeals to his vanity. Arragon, on the other hand, is attracted by the silver casket, because it promises to give him "as much as he deserves," and he holds a high opinion of his own merit. In the meantime Bassanio is making elaborate preparations for his expedition to Belmont; and at the same time Lorenzo is carrying on an intrigue which ends in his elopement with Jessica on the very night that Bassanio sets sail for Belmont. The fact that his daughter has eloped with a Christian, together with the loss of money and jewels which she has carried off, enrages Shylock beyond measure. Unhappily at this very time comes the rumour that one of Antonio's ships has been lost, and the friends of Antonio are uneasy at the thought that Shylock may attempt to revenge himself on Antonio for the loss of his money and jewels.

ACT III.—SCENE I.

This scene forms the natural sequel to Scene VIII. of the previous Act. We learn now for a certainty that Antonio has lost "A ship of rich lading," and we are given a hint (ll. 18-19) that this may not prove to be the end of his losses (ll. 90-91). At the same time we see very clearly the effect which the flight of Jessica is likely to have in intensifying Shylock's desire for revenge. When Shylock first prepared the bond it is doubtful whether he intended to do more than humiliate Antonio if he were given the opportunity; but now that he is driven to a frenzy by the news which Tubal has brought to him regarding Jessica, he resolves to "have the heart of him if he forfeit." This is one of the most dramatic scenes in the play, and without this scene it would be difficult to understand the motives of Shylock in actually insisting upon the forfeit of the pound of flesh.

2. it lives there unchecked. The report has not been denied.

4. the Goodwins. Famous shallows about twenty-five square miles in extent, off the coast of Kent. These sand-banks are said to have been formed during the reign of William the Conqueror, when the sea overflowed part of the estates of Earl Godwin.

6-7. my gossip Report. Rumour is represented as a talkative old woman.

9. knapped. Gnawed, nibbled.

11. without any slips of prolixity. Without forgetting myself and going into tedious details.

crossing the plain highway of talk. Wandering away from the subject instead of going straight to the point.

15. the full stop. Come to the end of your story.

27. the wings. The boy's clothing.

29. **complexion.**   Nature, disposition.

34. **Rhenish.**   White in colour.

37. **match.**   Bargain.

38. **prodigal.**   Ready to lend his money so freely to his friends.

39. **smug.**   Self-satisfied.

40. **mart.**   Exchange, money-market.

51. **dimensions.**   Physical size.

52. **affections.**   Feelings.

60. **what is his humility?**   What kind of meekness does he show?

61. **sufferance.**   Endurance.

63. I shall do my best to improve upon this teaching.

but.   If not.

75. **Frankfort.**   In Germany; famous for its fairs.

76. **The curse.**   The reference is probably to one of the several curses in the Old Testament, which are pronounced upon the children of Israel if they fail to keep the Law.   See *Leviticus*, xxvi., 33-39; also *Deuteronomy*, xxviii., 15-68.

79. **hearsed.**   In her coffin.

81. **Why, so.**   It's just what I might have expected.

102. **divers.**   Several.

108. **for a monkey.**   In payment for a monkey that she had bought.

110. **turquoise.**   A precious stone, blue in colour, and supposed to possess certain mysterious virtues.   For instance it was supposed to brighten or fade according to the health of the wearer.

Leah.   Shylock's dead wife.

115. **fee me an officer.**   Engage an officer to arrest Antonio when the bond falls due.

118. **synagogue.**   The Jewish place of worship.

QUESTIONS.

1. Judging from what Shylock says in this scene, what were his motives in wishing to torture Antonio?

2. "In the course of this scene the dramatist puts into the mouth of Shylock a passionate plea for justice to the Jewish people."

(a) Sum up this plea briefly in your own words.

(b) Point out any rhetorical devices which the dramatist has used in order to strengthen his plea.

3. What significance do you attach to the fact that Antonio is *at his house* and has sent for his friends?

4. In the case of each of the following passages show the dramatic significance of the italicized expressions:—

(a) Antonio, as I heard in Genoa, hath an argosy cast away, *coming from Tripolis.*

(b) There came *divers of Antonio's creditors* in my company to Venice.

(c) It was my turquoise; *I had it of Leah when I was a bachelor.*

(d) Go, go, Tubal, and meet me *at our synagogue.*

SCENE II.

The greater part of Scene II. has to do with Bassanio's choice of the caskets, a detailed study of which will be found in the Introduction, page xx. To make the pleasure of the audience at Bassanio's success all the more complete we learn now for the first time, that the fortunes of Gratiano and Nerissa depended likewise upon Bassanio's choice; and this two-fold connection, as we shall see later, contributes a good deal to our enjoyment of the final scenes in the play. The fortunes of Bassanio have now reached their highest point; and as if to make the situation more dramatic by contrast with Bassanio's happiness, at this moment Salerio arrives, in company with Lorenzo and Jessica, bearing the ill-news that Antonio's ships have all been lost and that his bond to the Jew is forfeit. It now becomes necessary for Bassanio to explain the situation to Portia, and it is to her that the audience now naturally turns for a solution of the difficulties of the play.

6. Hate does not give advice of that kind.

8. A maiden cannot speak what she thinks.

11. **I am then forsworn.** I should then have **broken my oath.**

14. **Beshrew.** A plague upon.

15. **o'erlooked.** Bewitched, cast a spell.

18. **naughty.** Wicked.

21. Let fortune take the blame for it.

22. **peize.** Literally, to weigh down; hence, to retard, to make it go more slowly.

23. **To eke it.** To add to it, to increase it.

26-8. The rack was a wooden frame upon which prisoners were stretched and tortured. This was a common method of punishment in the case of those who were suspected of treason.

29. **mistrust.** Fear that I shall choose wrongly.

30. **fear the enjoying.** Fear lest I shall not enjoy.

34. **enforced.** Forced to confess.

anything. Anything, whether true or not, which may put an end to their torture.

38. **Had been the very sum.** Would have summed up completely.

46. **a swan-like end.** A reference to the old belief that the swan sang before its death.

53-5. It was at one time the custom for musicians, hired for the occasion, to awaken the bridegroom on his wedding day by playing under his window.

dulcet. Sweet.

55-63. According to the Greek myth, Laomedon, king of Troy, had offended Poseidon (Neptune) the god of the sea; whereupon Poseidon sent a sea-monster to ravage the coasts. When the Trojans consulted the oracle they were advised to try to appease Poseidon by sacrificing one of their maidens to the monster. The lot fell upon Hesione, the daughter of Laomedon, and she was about to be sacrificed when Hercules appeared on the scene. He offered to slay the monster and rescue Hesione, on condition that Laomedon should give him as a reward the horses which Tros, the father of Laomedon, had received from Zeus. Hercules slew the monster as he had agreed, but Laomedon failed to keep his promise and was afterwards slain by Hercules.

56. **no less presence.** As noble a bearing.

much more love.   Hercules rescued Hesione only for the sake of the reward.

57. **Alcides.**   See note on Act II., Scene I., l. 36.

58. **howling.**   Weeping, lamenting.

59. **I stand for sacrifice.**   I represent the victim, Hesione.

60. **Dardanian.** Trojan. Dardanus was the mythical ancestor of the Trojans.

61. **bleared.**   Tear-stained.

65. **fancy.**   The kind of love that is little more than a passing fancy.

66. **Or . . . or.**   Whether . . . or.

69-71.   When we fall in love with some person or thing merely because it is pleasing to the eye, our love will not last long.

75. **So.**   Referring to the idea of the song.

least themselves.   What Bassanio means to say is that objects are sometimes in reality quite different from what the outward shows would seem to indicate.   They cannot be depended on.

76. **still.**   Always, constantly.

77-9.   An advocate with a pleasing voice is able to conceal much of the evil in the case which he is pleading.   The grammatical construction is confused.   As it stands, *But* (that not), which stands for *plea*, is the subject of *obscures*: but in reality it is the "gracious voice" that "obscures the show of evil."

80. **sober brow.**   Grave-looking divine.

81. **approve it.**   Prove it, justify it.

83. **so simple.**   So thoroughly and entirely a vice.

but assumes.   That it does not assume; as not to assume.

84. **his.**   Its.

85. **all.**   Quite, altogether.

87. **Mars.**   The god of War.

88. **have livers white as milk.**   Are cowards.   Red blood was considered a sign of courage.

89. **valour's excrement.**   The outward appearance of courage.

excrement.   Outgrowth, referring to the beard.

90. **To render them redoubted.** To make them objects of fear.

91. A reference to false hair, which was sold by weight.

93. **lightest.** Most giddy or frivolous in character; also lighted in colour because the locks of hair were "golden."

95. **wanton.** Playful.

96. **fairness.** Beauty.

known. Completes *are* and refers to *locks*.

97. **dowry.** Literally, the goods which a wife brings to her husband as a marriage portion. Here, the property which belonged to another person's head.

98. A nominative absolute construction.

99. **guiled.** Treacherous.

100. **scarf.** Kerchief, head-dress.

101. **an Indian beauty.** Dark hair and complexion were in disfavour in Shakespeare's time, perhaps because Queen Elizabeth was fair-complexioned. Hence the Indian beauty with dark hair and swarthy skin would be considered ugly, according to Elizabethan standards.

104. **Midas.** In return for a service which Midas, king of Phrygia, had performed, Dionysius (Bacchus) agreed to grant him any favour which he might ask. Midas in his greed for wealth asked that everything he touched might turn to gold. Dionysius granted his request; but to the dismay of Midas even the food which he touched turned into gold and he was in danger of starving to death. He begged Dionysius to take back his favour, and he was told to bathe in the river Pactolus. As a result he was restored to his former condition, but the sand of the river thereafter was mixed with gold.

105. **drudge.** Coins are made of silver, and it is compared to a servant who does the drudgery of business.

106. **meagre.** Poor, having nothing to make it attractive.

110. **fleet to air.** Quickly vanish.

111. **rash-embraced.** To which I yielded too quickly.

112. **green-eyed.** Because of a jealous disposition are said to be sickly and jaundiced in appearance.

118. **counterfeit.** Likeness.

118-9. This portrait is so lifelike that it seems as if the painter had nearly created another Portia.

128. to steal both his. To hold him fascinated so that he could not look away from it to paint the other eye.

129. unfurnish'd. Without the other eye as a companion.

129-22. Just as my praise fails to do justice to the picture, so the picture fails to do justice to the real Portia.

133. continent. That which contains it.

135. You that are so fortunate in the risk you have taken, and that choose as truly as you have done.

139. And consider (hold) your fortune to be a happy one.

142. gentle. Kind.

143. by note. As directed in the scroll.

159. livings. Worldly possessions.

161. to term in gross. To state at its gross value.

170. converted. Made over, changed.

but now. Only a moment ago.

176. presage. Foretell.

177. It will be my privilege to complain of you.

179. I cannot express my feelings in words, but my blood runs faster in my veins.

184-6. It is impossible to hear what the separate individuals are saying; you can hear only the pleased "buzzing" of the multitude.

186. Expressed in the confused buzzing, but not expressed in distinct words.

194. from me. There is a play on words here. On the surface Gratiano says "You do not need any good wishes from me," but he means, no doubt, "You cannot by wishing take any joy *away from* me."

198. so. If.

203-4. Delay (intermission) is not one of my qualities any more than it is yours.

205. stood. Depended.

208. roof. Roof of my mouth.

209. if promise last.   If Nerissa holds to her promise.

220. infidel.   His Jewish bride.

221. Salerio.   There are some critics who argue that Shakespeare was not likely to introduce a new character at this stage in the play, and that *Salerio* is probably a misprint for *Salanio*. But *Salerio* appears in all the early editions of the play.

223-4.   If I have the right to bid you welcome to a household in which I myself have so recently been given an interest.

236. Commends him to you.   Sends his salutations.

241. estate.   Condition.

245. royal.   Both noble and wealthy, like a king.

247. the Jasons.   See note on Act I., Scene II., ll. 175-8.

250. shrewd.   Sharp, unpleasant; literally, accursed.

254. constitution.   Disposition, temper of mind.

255. constant.   Self-controlled.

271. mere.   Absolute, thorough.   In modern English *mere* is used only in speaking of petty, trifling things.

272. To feed my means.   To furnish myself with money.

276. hit.   Success.   Or *hit* may be a participle. "Has not one hit the mark?"

278. Barbary.   The Barbary States in the north of Africa.

286. confound.   Ruin.

287. plies.   Urges, presses his case.

288. impeach.   Lay a charge against.   In England many towns and cities held charters from the king granting them freedom upon certain conditions.   For the purpose of his story Shakespeare speaks of Venice as if it were an English town which had been granted a charter upon condition that the rights of aliens would be respected; and Shylock threatens that if justice is denied to him he will bring action to have the charter taken away.   But as a matter of history Venice was a free, self-governed state, and the freedom of the city did not depend upon a charter from any higher power.

290-1. magnificoes of greatest port.   The nobles of greatest importance.

292. envious.   Malicious.

303. Supply *most* before "unwearied."

308. **For me.** On my account.

323. **cheer.** Countenance.

333. **dispatch.** Hasten, as distinguished from *despatch*, meaning either to send off, or to execute.

QUESTIONS.

1. Portia says to Bassanio, "I pray you tarry; pause a day or two before you choose."

(*a*) Why does she wish him to pause?

(*b*) Why is he not willing to do so?

2. (*a*) Show clearly what bearing the song has upon the choice of the caskets.

(*b*) The charge is sometimes made that Portia by means of this song gave Bassanio a clue as to which was the right casket. How would you answer this charge?

3. (*a*) On what occasion earlier in the play has Bassanio been warned against trusting to the "outward shows" of things?

(*b*) "The world is still deceived with ornament." Bassanio attempts to prove this by citing four different examples. Enumerate them.

(*c*) What is there in (i) the inscription, and (ii) the leaden casket itself, that leads Bassanio to choose it?

4. One might suppose that Portia would be somewhat displeased, if not shocked, to find that Bassanio was in debt and that it would require the immediate payment of at least three thousand ducats to meet Antonio's obligations to Shylock. How has Shakespeare provided against this difficulty?

SCENE III.

In the "Borrowing Scene" in Act I. when Shylock reproaches Antonio with the indignities which he has heaped upon him in the past, Antonio replies·

"I am as like to call thee so again,
To spit on thee again, to spurn thee too."

And though our sympathies are, as a whole, with Antonio, yet we cannot help feeling that Shylock has been treated unjustly. In this scene Shylock has his revenge, and the once proud Antonio is driven to beg mercy of his hated enemy. Yet while we feel that he has himself brought these misfortunes on his own head our sympathies are aroused in his behalf and we are reminded (ll. 24-26) that Shylock's hatred is due to other causes than the mere desire to revenge the indignities that he has suffered.

This scene is, in a sense, a preparation for the Trial Scene to follow. Shylock, we see, is relentless. Antonio himself admits that "the duke cannot deny the course of law," and for the moment our only hope lies in the arrival of Bassanio, who is in a position to make a further appeal to the avarice of the Jew.

11. **naughty.** Good-for-nothing.

fond. Foolish.

16. **dull-eyed.** Stupid.

20. **It.** The neuter pronoun is used to express contempt.

impenetrable. No appeals have any effect on him.

21. **kept.** Lived, dwelt.

25. **forfeitures.** Penalties for non-payment.

31-3. These lines present difficulty. As it stands, *commodity* must be taken to mean "advantages," or "privileges," and in this case it is the denial of these privileges that will call in question the freedom of the state. *It* (l. 32) thus refers to *commodity*. Some editors, however, prefer to write the passage with a comma after *law* (l. 30), and a colon or semicolon after *Venice*, and to substitute *'Twill* for *Will* (l. 33). The meaning then is "the duke cannot deny the course of law on account of the trade (commodity) that strangers have with us in Venice. If it (the course of law) be denied, it will cast a doubt upon the freedom of the state."

commodity. Either *privileges* or *trade*, according to the punctuation.

34-5. The trade from which the city gains its profit is carried on with all nations.

36. **bated.** Reduced me in flesh.

QUESTIONS.

1. By reference to Act I., Scene III., and Act III., Scene I., as well as to the present scene, show clearly what Shylock's different motives were in insisting on his bond.

2. Antonio himself has not appeared in the play since the departure of Bassanio (Act II., Scene VI.). Upon what occasions has he been referred to in the meantime?

SCENE IV.

The chief purpose of this scene is to give the audience some necessary information relative to the plans of Portia and Nerissa. Lorenzo and Jessica are to be left in charge of Portia's house during her absence; Balthasar is despatched to Padua with a letter in which Portia asks her cousin Bellario for a legal opinion on Antonio's case; and Portia playfully discloses to Nerissa her plan to set out for Venice in disguise in order to be present at the trial of Antonio.

2-3. You have a true and noble understanding of the highest kind of friendship.

9. Than your ordinary goodness of heart would lead you to be.

12. **waste.** Spend, pass.

13. Just as the yoke, in the case of oxen, is borne equally by both and at the same time holds them together, so love, in the case of two friends, is shared equally and forms a bond which unites them more closely.

14. **needs.** Of necessity. The genitive of the noun *need* has survived with this adverbial use.

a like proportion. A similarity. It is doubtful whether Shakespeare meant to say that the similarity was to be in proportion to the love, or whether the qualities of the one companion were to be in proportion to the same qualities in the other.

15. **lineaments.** The idea seems to be that where two people think and act alike, even the lines of their faces will at length come to bear a resemblance. *Lineaments* in Shakespeare's time was, however, used in speaking of the limbs as well as of the features.

20. the semblance of my soul. If what Portia has just said is true, then Antonio must closely resemble Bassanio, whom she refers to as her "soul" because he is as dear to her as her very soul.

20-1. There is a reference here to the deliverance of souls from purgatory.

22. This. This reference to what I have done.

25. husbandry. Care.

manage. Management.

33. imposition. The duty that is imposed upon you.

54. notes. Bearing upon Antonio's case.

garments. To be used in disguising themselves for the trial.

55. imagined speed. All the speed imaginable.

56. tranect. Some editions have *traject*. Both words are used of the ferry.

57. trades. Passes back and forth.

64. habit. Dress.

65-6. They shall think we possess the qualities of men, in which we are lacking.

69. braver grace. More gallant manner.

71. a reed voice. A shrill piping voice.

mincing. Delicate, with a show of affectation.

73. quaint. Ingenious, artful.

76. I could not do withal. An idiomatic expression meaning "I could not do anything to help it."

78. puny. Petty.

81. raw. Crude, clumsy.

Jacks. Fellows,—a term of contempt.

QUESTIONS.

1. "Our good opinion of Antonio is due not so much to what he himself says and does as to what his most intimate friends say of him." In addition to what Lorenzo says of Antonio in this scene, refer to other occasions in the play in which Antonio's friends speak of his good qualities.

2. In order that Portia might appear in the court in disguise and conduct the case in behalf of Antonio, why was it necessary that she should consult her cousin, Doctor Bellario?

Scene V.

This scene does not contribute anything to the development of the plot: but it provides relaxation for the audience, and at the same time it helps to give the impression that a sufficient interval of time has passed to enable Portia and Nerissa to reach Venice before the Trial Scene begins.

1. Yes, truly.   In answer to some remark of Jessica's.

3. I fear you.   I am concerned as to what will come of you.

4. agitation.   Cogitation.

14-5.   Scylla and Charybdis were two rocks between Italy and Sicily.   Upon the rock nearest to Italy dwelt Scylla, a fearful monster; upon the other rock dwelt Charybdis, who thrice every day swallowed the waters of the sea and thrice threw them up again.   The rocks were separated only by a narrow channel, through which ships had to pass; and in trying to avoid the one monster they were in danger of falling a prey to the other.

16. gone.   Lost.

23. rasher.   A thin slice of bacon.

29. are out.   Have quarrelled.

34-5.   The best quality of wit will be silence; that is, the wittiest person will be he who keeps silence.

38. stomachs.   Appetites.

41-4.   Launcelot plays upon the two meanings of *cover*,—to lay the cloth, and to put on one's hat.

44. my duty.   To keep my head uncovered in presence of my superiors.

45. quarrelling with occasion.   Taking a contrary meaning out of everything that happens to be said.

52. humours and conceits.   Whims and fancies.

54. discretion.   He calls upon discretion, or good judgment, because Launcelot has shown none of it in the use of his words.

suited.   That is, ill-suited to the sense.

57. A many fools.   A multitude of fools.   In older English *many* was sometimes used as a noun.

in better place.   In higher rank in life.

58. Garnish'd like him. This may mean, furnished with a supply of words such as he has; but the more probable meaning is, furnished with as little discretion as he has.

a tricksy word. A word upon which they can pun.

59. Defy the matter. Disregard the sense.

How cheers't thou? What cheer? How are you faring?

66. mean it. Mean to live an upright life. Some editors prefer the reading *merit it*.

71. Pawn'd. Thrown in as an additional state.

rude. Because there are few women such as Portia.

72. fellow. Equal.

77. stomach. A play on the word:—appetite for my dinner and inclination to praise her.

81. set you forth. Give you your character.

QUESTIONS.

1. When did Launcelot last appear in the play? Why is he introduced at this point in the play?

2. (*a*). What purpose does this scene serve in the play?

(*b*). What impression do you get of Lorenzo from this scene?

SUMMARY OF ACT III.

In the beginning of Act III. we learn that the report as to the loss of one of Antonio's ships has been confirmed; and in this same scene Tubal brings news of the loss of still another. Shylock, too, has heard further particulars regarding his daughter's flight, and he is alternately swayed by grief at his own losses and by desire for revenge upon Antonio. In the meantime, to the great joy of Portia, Bassanio has been successful in his choice of the caskets; but in the midst of his rejoicing, he receives word that the three months have expired and that Antonio's bond has become forfeit. Portia at once offers Bassanio money "to pay the petty debt twenty times over," and urges him to make haste to Venice. No sooner is he gone than she conceives the bold plan of going to Venice herself to act as judge in place of her cousin, the learned Bellario, who has been sent for to try the case. She keeps her plan secret, and after installing Lorenzo and Jessica in charge of the house and sending a message to Bellario, she and Nerissa set out for Venice. The Act closes with a glimpse into Portia's household in her absence. In this closing scene our attention is for the moment diverted from the more serious matters in hand; and at the same time we are given the impression that sufficient time has elapsed to enable Portia to reach Venice in time for the opening of the trial.

Act IV.—Scene I.

The Trial Scene opens upon a crowded court-room; for the unusual case of Shylock and Antonio has attracted widespread attention. We have been prepared in previous scenes for the course which Shylock intends to follow. We know that, whatever may happen, he is determined to exact the forfeiture, and that no appeals for mercy from the Duke or from Antonio's friends can turn him from his purpose. But we are interested, nevertheless, in the arguments by which he is able to meet these appeals.

With the entrance of Portia the case at once assumes a new interest, for it is to Portia as judge that the audience must now look for the deliverance of Antonio. But, as we might have expected, Shylock takes his stand more firmly than ever upon his rights under the Venetian charter, and upon the conditions of the bond itself. As the trial proceeded it must have seemed to those who were looking on, as if Antonio's case were becoming more hopeless every moment; for Shylock rejects in turn Portia's appeals to his mercy and to his avarice, and when he takes his stand upon the strict letter of the law and the strict wording of the bond, he is upheld by Portia. But when the crisis at length comes, the reasons for Portia's action at once becomes clear to us. She has in the first place forced Shylock to declare his purpose in such a way as to make it apparent that it is Antonio's life rather than strict justice that he is seeking; and to this situation the old Venetian law which every one but the learned Bellario had forgotten, is found to apply. She has in the second place driven Shylock to demand the fulfilment of the strict letter of the bond, and in so doing she has opened up a way of escape for Antonio. For since

Shylock takes his stand upon "the very words" of the bond
he can have no ground of complaint when Portia in turn
insists that he shall have "nothing but the forfeiture."

It is a question whether or not Shakespeare intended the
audience to feel any pity for Shylock when he leaves the
court at the close of the trial scene; but it must not be forgotten that to an Elizabethan audience at least, the misfortunes of Shylock still had their compensations. His life had
been spared by the Duke; he was still left in possession of half
of his goods, while the whole of his property was to go to
Lorenzo and Jessica upon his death; and, better than all else,
he had been forced to turn Christian and might now hope for
salvation in accordance with the Christian faith.

1. **What.** An exclamation intended to call the court to order.

5. **Uncapable.** Incapable.

6. **From.** Of.

dram. Particle; a dram is a very small weight.

7. **qualify.** Moderate, soften.

8. **rigorous course.** Harsh course of action.

9. **that.** Since.

10. **envy.** Malice.

13. **tyranny.** Relentless cruelty.

his. His spirit.

16. **Make room.** The court-room is crowded.

17-19. It is thought that you are carrying out your malice in
this fashion only till you reach the final stage in the action.

20. **remorse.** Pity.

21. **apparent.** Seeming.

24. **loose the forfeiture.** Let the penalty go unclaimed.

26. **moiety.** A portion.

28. **huddled.** Crowded together.

29. **Enow.** Enough.

30. **commiseration of his state.** Pity for his condition.

33. **offices.** Duties.

35. **possess'd.** Informed.

38-9. See note on Act III., Scene II., ll. 288-9.

41. **carrion.** Dead, decaying.

43. **humour.** Whim.

46. **ban'd.** Destroyed, poisoned.

47. **a gaping pig.** A reference to the custom of serving a roast pig at table upon feast days, with a lemon or a roasted apple in its open (gaping) mouth.

49-51. In Shakespeare's time the word *affection* was used with reference to the effect which an object produced upon the senses. The sight of a gaping pig, for instance, produced a feeling of displeasure. The word *passion*, on the other hand, was used to refer only to the feelings, without reference to the senses. The passage then means, "Our feelings (passions) are swayed in one direction or another according as an object pleases or displeases our senses."

55. **woollen.** The woollen covering of the bagpipe.

56-7. He himself is annoyed by the sight of the offensive object; and in showing his dislike for it he gives annoyance to other people.

59. **lodged.** Settled. **certain.** Fixed.

63. **current.** Course.

66-70. Bassanio says "Even if you do hate Antonio, you need not go so far as to kill him." Shylock replies, "If you *hate* any one, you *do* want to kill him. Otherwise you do not hate him." "But," answers Bassanio, "A man may wrong you without your *hating* him in that way. Hatred does not come all at once." To this Shylock retorts, "You surely would not give your enemy a chance to wrong you a second time?"

71. **think you question.** Remember that you are arguing.

74. **the main flood.** The ocean.

bate. Fall short of, decrease.

78. **no noise.** Any noise.

79. **fretten.** Fretted, disturbed.

84. As briefly and as plainly as is convenient to the court.

89. **draw them.** Take them from the bag which Bassanio is holding out.

92-3.   Shylock assumes that when he is acting within his legal rights he cannot be doing any wrong.

96.   You use in the performance of base, menial duties.

101. **such.**   Such as you enjoy.

108. **Upon my power.**   In accordance with my authority as duke.

120. **tainted.**   Touched by disease.

wether.   A young (male) sheep.

131.   The suggestion is that Shylock's *soul* is as hard as his *sole*.

132. **hangman.**   Executioner.

134. **envy.**   Malice.

135. **wit.**   Cleverness.

136. **inexorable.**   Unrelenting, merciless.   Another reading is *inexecrable*, meaning, "too bad for cursing."

137.   Justice is to blame for letting you live at all.

139. **Pythagoras.**   A Greek philosopher and mathematician who lived about 520 B.C.   He is said to have preached the doctrine of transmigration of souls.

142-3.   The grammatical construction is confused.

147.   Till you can destroy the legality of my bond by your scolding.

166. **bettered.**   Improved.

168-9. **at my importunity.**   At my urgent request.

to fill up.   To comply with.

170. **to let him lack.**   Such as would cause him to lack.

172-3. **whose trial,** etc.   This test to which he is put will show the praise he deserves, better than my words.

179. **difference.**   Dispute.

180.   That keeps this case before the court.

184.   Merely a formal question to introduce the case.

187. **in such rule.**   In such regular form.

188. **impugn.**   Oppose.

189. **danger.**   A legal term meaning "power to harm."

191. **confess the bond.**   Admit that it is genuine.

194.   How can I be compelled?

195.   Mercy, by its very nature is not a forced (strained) quality, which you can compel a man to show.

201-3.   The king's sceptre is a symbol of his earthly power upon which depends his awe and majesty which makes him feared and dreaded by his subjects.

201. **sceptre.**   The staff or mace which is the symbol of royal authority.

temporal.   Here, worldy, earthly.

202. **The attribute to.**   The quality that is essential to.

208. **seasons.**   Moderates, tempers.

217. **My deeds upon my head.**   I am willing to suffer the consequences of my deeds. I do not need the mercy you speak of.

225. **That malice bears down truth.**   That Shylock's malice is stronger than his desire for justice.

truth.   Honesty of purpose.

226.   Force the law to give way to your authority.

234.   **A Daniel.**   A reference to a Hebrew book entitled *Susannah and the Elders*, in which Daniel is represented as having delivered a woman suffering under a false accusation.

242. **Why.**   This word does not express surprise: it is equivalent to some such expression as " 'Tis true."

247. **tenour.**   The conditions contained in it.

260-1.   The law does not mention a case exactly like this: but the law is intended to cover all such cases, even though the penalty is an unusual one.

272-3. **on your charge.**   At your expense.

280. **arm'd.**   With fortitude.

284. **use.**   Custom.

290. **process.**   Manner.

291. **speak me fair.**   Speak well of me.

297. **with all my heart.**   Note the play on words.

299. **Which.**   *Which* was formerly used to refer to either persons or things.

314. **the stock of Barrabas.**   The descendants of Barrabas, even though he was a robber and a murderer.   See *Matthew*, xxvii., 16.

316. **pursue sentence.**   Follow with the judgment.

324. **A sentence!**   An excellent judgment.

327. **jot.**   The smallest particle.   From the Greek *iota*, the name of the letter *i*, the smallest letter in the alphabet.

332. **confiscate.**   Confiscated.

352. **a just pound.**   An exact pound.

356. **estimation.**   Value, weight.

371. **stay.**   Wait for.

question.   Argument.

379. **seize.**   Take possession of; a legal term.

380. **privy coffer.**   Money which was not part of the public funds used in the administration of government.

privy.   Private.

coffer.   Treasury.

382. **'gainst all other voice.**   No one else having the right to pardon him.

383. **predicament.**   Situation, plight.

400.   Portia wishes to make sure that Antonio's share is not to be interfered with.

409. **To quit.**   To give up.

411. **in use.**   That is, Antonio is to have the use of the money during Shylock's lifetime; and upon Shylock's death it is to be handed over to Lorenzo.

419. **recant.**   Recall, take back.

433.   I desire pardon of your grace.   This idiom was common in Shakespeare's time.

437. **gratify.**   Reward.

443. **cope.**   Requite.   **withal.**   With.

450. **know me.**   Recognize me; remember me.

452.   I am compelled to try to persuade you.

454. **as a tribute.**   As a mark of your esteem.

482. **An if.** *An* is a shortened form of *and*, meaning *if*. As used here it strengthens the force of *if*.

487. **withal.** Besides, in addition.

QUESTIONS.

1. In ll. 6-8 Antonio says, "I have heard your grace hath ta'en great pains to qualify his rigorous cause." Refer to a previous passage in the play in which the Duke's efforts in behalf of Shylock are mentioned.

2. (*a*) What arguments does the Duke put forth in the attempt to influence Shylock (ll. 16-34, and ll. 90-91)?

(*b*) State briefly in your own words Shylock's answer in each case.

3. (*a*) Compare the attitude of Antonio towards Shylock in this scene with that of Gratiano.

(*b*) How do you account for Antonio's apparent resignation to his fate?

4. Portia first appeals to Shylock's mercy, then to his avarice,—then to both together. What answer does Shylock make to each of these appeals?

5. Point out the different expressions in the scene that help to show Portia's attitude towards the Venetian law.

6. What is Portia's real purpose in asking Shylock to provide a surgeon lest Antonio should bleed to death?

7. What is the dramatic purpose of the speeches of Bassanio and Gratiano in ll. 298-311?

8. "Portia really upsets the bond upon a quibble; for it is unreasonable to suppose that a pound of flesh does not include the blood that goes with it, and it is unreasonable to expect that Shylock would be able to cut off an exact pound." Point out the special circumstances of the case that make this quibble of Portia's appear reasonable.

9. In ll. 342, 361, 370, and 424-6, Shylock successively modifies his demands. Show definitely the reason for his changed attitude in each case.

SCENE II.

This short scene is necessary to give us some idea of the plans of Portia and Nerissa, and to prepare the way for the Rings' Episode in the final scene of the play.

6. you are well o'erta'en. I am glad I have overtaken you.

7. upon more advice. Upon further consideration.

19. old swearing. Plenty of swearing. *Old* was used frequently in Shakespeare's time as an intensive.

21. outface them. Put on a bolder face; shame them.

23. tarry. Wait for you.

24. shew me. Conduct me.

QUESTION.

In the preceding scene Shylock had said, "Send the deed after me and I will sign it." How has the dramatist turned this circumstance to account in the present scene in furthering the action of the play?

SUMMARY OF ACT IV.

In the middle of Act III. the problem of the choice of the caskets was successfully solved; but at the same time the crisis in the bond story was also reached. As we saw in the early part of the play, Bassanio's success was made possible only by the fact that Antonio was willing to undertake the risk of signing the bond. It seems only fitting, then, that as Bassanio has indirectly been the cause of bringing Antonio into this difficulty, he should, if possible, be the means of relieving him from it. Now it happens that in choosing the right casket he has made it possible for Portia to come to the assistance of Antonio, he thus provides the means, indirectly, for Antonio's relief. Practically the whole of Act IV. is devoted to the Trial Scene, and throughout the trial the chief interest of the audience lies in Portia's conduct of the case. (See introduction to Scene I.). Indeed so well does Portia act her part as judge that for the time being, the real Portia is forgotten; but no sooner is the trial over than the other side of her nature reasserts itself, and in her playful efforts to get her husband's ring the gayer and brighter side of the real Portia again reappears.

Act V.—Scene I.

This scene is not essential to the action of the play, but it
provides relief from the intense emotions of the Trial Scene
which preceded it and helps to bring the play to a 'happy
ending.' The Rings' Episode forms the chief interest in the
scene, and as a background for this humorous situation we
have the beautiful grounds of Portia's mansion bathed in soft
moonlight, and gentle strains of music, with which Lorenzo has
planned to welcome Portia home. And when the storm which
Portia and Nerissa have raised about their rings has blown
over, there is good news in store for Antonio, and "manna"
for the unthrifty Lorenzo, and a happy reunion for the lovers
who have been so rudely separated by the misfortunes of
Antonio.

5-7. Troilus was one of the sons of Priam, king of Troy.
Cressida, according to one version of the story, was a Grecian
maiden who was taken prisoner by the Trojans. She and
Troilus fell in love, and swore to be faithful to each other,
whatever might befall. In the course of time Cressida was
exchanged by the Trojans for another prisoner, and was taken
back to the Grecian camp. Here she met with Diomede, and
forgetting her vows to Troilus she became enamoured of the
Greek youth.

9-11. Pyramus and Thisbe were two Babylonish lovers.
Their parents would not allow them to see each other, and
they were forced to meet secretly. On one occasion they had
agreed to meet at the tomb of Ninus, outside the city walls.
Thisbe arrived first at the meeting-place, but was frightened
away by a lion. In her haste she dropped her mantle, and the
lion which had recently slain an ox, tore it with its bloody
jaws. When Pyramus reached the spot, seeing the blood-
stained mantle, he fancied that Thisbe had been slain, and in
his grief he took his own life. When Thisbe at length returned
and found Pyramus slain, she also killed herself.

13-5. In the course of his wanderings after the fall of Troy,
the Trojan hero Æneas came to the city of Carthage, in
Northern Africa. Dido, the Queen of Carthage, fell in love
with him; and so great was her grief and disappointment
when he sailed away from Carthage that she threw herself
upon a funeral pyre and perished in the flames.

13. a willow.   The emblem of unrequited love.

14. waft.   Waved.

17-8.   Medea was the daughter of Aëtes the king of Colchis. When Jason came to Colchis in search of the Golden Fleece, Medea fell in love with him, and it was through her aid that he was able to carry off the coveted fleece.   By means of the magic powers which she possessed she succeeded in restoring Aeson, the aged father of Jason, to youth.   As the story goes, she made a potion from enchanted herbs which she gathered by moonlight.   A part of this potion she gave Aeson to drink, and the other part she poured into a vein which she had opened in his neck.

20. steal.   Note the double meaning here.

21. unthrift love.   A spendthrift lover.

28. shrew.   A scolding woman.

30. out-night you.   Out-do you in talking of "such a night."

34-5.   Lorenzo makes fun of the self-importance of Stephano.

39. holy crosses.   Wayside crosses are very common in Italy.

48.   Launcelot is imitating the sound of a horn announcing the arrival of a courier or "post."

56. horn.   The post-horn, with perhaps a reference to a cornucopia, or horn of plenty.

58. expect.   Await.

61. signify.   Announce, make known.

67. Become.   Are suitable for.

69. patines.   A *patine* is a small gold plate used in celebrating the mass in the Roman Catholic church.   The stars here are compared to patines.

70-2.   A reference to the popular belief in "the music of the spheres."   Each star as it moves on its course makes sweet music, singing in harmony with the cherubim.

But.   A pronoun, equivalent to *which not.*

his.   Its.

quiring.   The same as *choiring*; singing.

young-eyed.   Either, youthful, fresh-faced, or with clear vision.

cherubins. The Hebrew plural of *cherub* is *cherubim.* The form *cherubins* is due to French influence.

73. The human soul, too, makes music, but while it (the soul) is inclosed in this coarse (gross) impure body we cannot hear the music.

vesture of decay. The body, which, is as it were, the garment in which the soul is dressed, and which is subject to decay.

76. **Diana.** The goddess of the moon. Lorenzo speaks of the moon as being asleep, perhaps because it is behind a cloud.

80. **attentive.** You are giving attention to the music, so that you have no chance to think of other things.

81. **wanton.** Unrestrained.

82. **unhandled.** Unbroken.

83. **Fetching.** Making.

87. **make a mutual stand.** Come to a stop, as if by common consent.

88. **savage.** Wild.

modest. Mild.

89. **the poet.** Probably the poet *Ovid*, who tells the story of Orpheus in his *Metamorphoses.*

90. **Orpheus.** The son of the muse Calliope. His music was so enchanting that the wild beasts, rocks, and trees moved from their places to the sound of his harp, and the rivers even flowed backwards in their course to hear him.

91. **stockish.** Dull and lifeless, like a block of wood.

92. **his.** Its.

95. **spoils.** Plundering, theft.

96. **The motions of his spirit.** The workings of his mind.

97. **Erebus.** The underworld; a place of darkness through which the spirits of the dead pass on their way to Hades.

101. **naughty.** Wicked.

106-7. **his state empties itself.** His splendour is no longer noticed.

108. **the main of waters.** The ocean.

109. **music.** Musicians.

110. **without respect.** Without reference to the circumstances which accompany it.

114. **attended.** Listened to with attention.

118-9. It is only when the time is suitable for us to see things at their best, that we are able to praise them rightly and realize what their true qualities are.

120. The moon is behind a cloud.

Endymion. A beautiful youth who fell into an endless sleep on the side of Mount Latmus. Selene (Diana), the goddess of the moon, was so charmed by his beauty that she came down and kissed him and lay by his side as he slept.

138. **tucket.** A flourish of trumpets.

145-6. While the people on the opposite side of the earth (the Antipodes) are having day, it is night here; but if *you* would walk abroad when the sun is no longer shining, it would still be day with us.

147. Note the quibble in *light* on the double sense of *bright* and *fickle*.

150. **sort.** Dispose.

160. Therefore I cut short this courtesy which consists merely in words.

168. **posy.** Another form of *poesy*; referring to the motto or verse inscribed on the inner side of the ring.

169. **cutler's poetry.** The mottoes inscribed on knife blades.

176. **respective.** Mindful that this was not an ordinary ring.

182. **scrubbed.** Stunted.

184. **prating.** Talkative.

189. **with faith.** With solemn promises.

225. **contain.** Keep.

230. **ceremony.** Sacred pledge.

234. **a civil doctor.** A doctor of civil law.

241. **courtesy.** The desire to show proper courtesy to him.

243. **besmear it.** Stain it.

244. **candles of the night.** Stars.

252. **advised.** Heedful.

263. **double.** Deceitful.

264. **an oath of credit.** An oath that can be trusted.

270. **Had quite miscarried.** Would have been wholly lost. *Miscarried* refers to *which*, i.e., *my body*.

272. **advisedly.** Deliberately.

287. **soon.** Quickly.

297. **living.** Something on which to live.

299. **road.** Harbour.

306. **manna.** See *Exodus*, xvi.

311. **charge us there upon inter'gatories.** A legal phrase. Make us take the oath to answer your questions (interrogatories) truly.

QUESTIONS.

1. (*a*) What evidences do you find in the play that **Lorenzo** possesses some sense of humour?

(*b*) It has been said of Lorenzo that he is of a dreamy, artistic temperament, but that at the same time he is inclined to be thriftless. Show by reference to the play what justification there is for this statement.

2. "Besides helping to provide a humorous ending for the play the Rings' Episode serves another important dramatic purpose." Explain.

3. Portia has thought it necessary to provide Bassanio and Gratiano with definite proof that she and Nerissa had acted the part of judge and judge's clerk respectively in the Trial Scene. What proof does she provide?

4. (*a*) Antonio returns to Belmont with Bassanio. Refer to the passage earlier in the play in which Portia expressed a wish that he should come.

(b) Portia has brought good news to Antonio. After all that has happened, Antonio's good fortune seems too good to be true. How is it that the audience is willing to credit Portia's announcement?

SUMMARY OF ACT V.

The main action of the play is complete at the close of the trial in Act IV., and the moonlight scene, together with the farcical situation of the Rings' Episode, are intended to relieve the feelings of the audience after the strain of the Trial Scene. It is in Act V., moreover, that Lorenzo appears in his true character—a dreamy artistic nature, whose poetical fancies are stirred by the sounds of music and the beauty of the moonlight night. Even if only for the fine poetical passages which it contains, this Act forms a delightful conclusion to the play.

QUESTIONS ON "THE MERCHANT OF VENICE"

FROM EXAMINATION PAPERS

**Senior High School Entrance, Senior Public School Diplomas,
and Entrance into the Model Schools**

1. *Lorenzo.* Madam, although I speak it in your presence,
    You have a noble and a true conceit
    Of god-like amity; which appears most strongly
    In bearing thus the absence of your lord.
    But if you knew to whom you show this honour,
    How true a gentleman you send relief,
    How dear a lover of my lord your husband,
    I know you would be prouder of the work
    Than customary bounty can enforce you.

(*a*) State briefly the circumstances which caused Lorenzo to address Portia as above.

(*b*) Describe the nature of the honour shown and the relief sent by Portia to which Lorenzo refers in lines 5 and 6.

(*c*) On what grounds does Portia explain her desire to aid thus an unknown person?

(*d*) How does Lorenzo chance to be in Portia's house at this time?

(*e*) Explain "true conceit" (l. 2); "god-like amity" (l. 3); "How dear a lover" (l. 7); "customary bounty" (l. 9).

2. By whom, and in what connection is each of the following passages spoken?

(*a*)   Had I but the means
    To hold a rival place with one of them,
    I have a mind presages me such thrift,
    That I should questionless be fortunate!

(*b*) If he will take it, so; if not, adieu;
    And, for my love, I pray you wrong me not.

(*c*)   Take this same letter,
    And use thou all the endeavour of a man
    In speed to Padua: see thou render this
    Into my cousin's hand.

(*d*) When she put it on she made me vow
  That I should neither sell nor give nor lose it.

3. State briefly your estimate of the character of Antonio, supporting your conclusions by references to the play.

4. *Shylock.* I have possess'd your grace of what I purpose
  And by our holy Sabbath have I sworn
  To have the due and forfeit of my bond:
  If you deny it, let the danger light
  Upon your charter and your city's freedom.
  You'll ask me, why I rather choose to have
  A weight of carrion flesh than to receive
  Three thousand ducats; I'll not answer that;
  But, say, it is my humour: is it answer'd?
  What if my house be troubled with a rat,
  And I be pleased to give ten thousand ducats
  To have it baned?

(*a*) To what remarks of the duke is Shylock here replying?

(*b*) Give the substance of Shylock's reply to the question suggested in the last three lines.

(*c*) Describe briefly the conduct of Gratiano during the trial.

(*d*) Explain: "possess'd" (l. 1); "our holy Sabbath" (l. 2); "your charter and your city's freedom" (l. 5).

5. Outline briefly the story of the caskets as given in *The Merchant of Venice.*

Junior Matriculation

1. (*a*) Give the substance of Portia's comment on each of any *three* of the different suitors named to her by Nerissa.

(*b*) What do we learn about Portia's character and ability from her comments on these suitors?

(*c*) State the terms of the sentence passed on Shylock. Discuss the justice of each of these terms.

2. (*a*) Give in your own words the arguments by which Portia tries to persuade the Jew to be merciful.

(*b*) Why have these arguments no effect on Shylock?

(c) Name the four separate stories that Shakespeare uses in *The Merchant of Venice*.

(d) Show very briefly how he has woven them into one unified story.

3. (a) What are the various causes of Shylock's hatred of Antonio?

(b) By what means does Shakespeare preserve our sympathy for Shylock in spite of his blood-thirstiness?

4. (a)   I speak too long; but 'tis to *peize* the time
              To *eke* it, and to draw it out in length,
              To stay you from election.

Who is the speaker, and to whom are the lines addressed? Explain the italicized expressions.

(b)   In such a night
              Stood Dido with a willow in her hand
              Upon the wild sea-banks.

Under what circumstances are these lines spoken? Who was Dido? Why is she represented "with a willow in her hand"?

5. (a)   Gentlemen,
              Will you prepare you for this masque to-night?
              I am provided of a torch-bearer.

Who is the speaker? To whom does he refer in the last line? What is the meaning of "masque"?

(b) . . . . . for in companions
              That do converse and *waste the time together*,
              Whose souls do *bear an equal yoke of love*,
              There must be *needs* a like *proportion*
              Of *lineaments*, of manners, and of spirit.

Who is the speaker? What companions does the speaker have in mind in making the statement? Explain the italicized expressions.

6. What purpose is served in the play by the introduction of Jessica? Indicate the three chief occasions on which she appears on the stage, and tell what she says and does on each of these occasions.

7. Give in detail the substance of what each of the three suitors says in arriving at a decision as to which casket to choose.

8. Give in not more than twenty lines the substance of either the opening scene in *The Merchant of Venice* or the Trial scene.

9. Name four of Portia's suitors who fail to try the test of the caskets. Give one characteristic of each, preferably in Portia's own words.

Entrance into the Normal Schools

1. Give, in order, the various stages in Portia's management of the case against Shylock in the Trial scene.

2. What purpose does each of the following serve in the development of the play:

(a) The conversation between Portia and Nerissa in Act I.

(b) The conversation between Shylock and Tubal in Act III.

(c) The incident of the rings.

3. Give the reasons that governed the choice of the caskets by Morocco *or* Arragon *or* Bassanio.

4. (a) Describe the means provided by Portia's father to test her suitors.

(b) Give the reasons of the three chief suitors for their respective choices.

(c) Show whether the interpretation of each proves the wisdom of the test.

(d) Describe the treatment of Shylock by his household and friends.

5. (a) State Shylock's motives in exacting the pound of flesh, and any circumstances found in the play that would influence him in so doing.

(b) What induced a good business man like Antonio to sign such a bond?

(c) Explain Portia's method of conducting the case in the Trial scene.

6. (a) Carefully outline the drift of the conversation of Bassanio, Shylock, and Antonio, in *The Merchant of Venice*, Act I., Scene 3, the scene of the negotiations for the loan.

(*b*) Point out details of the scene that serve to leave the impression that Antonio is running a serious risk in signing such a bond as Shylock proposes.

7. Mention the purposes served in the play by Launcelot.

8. Give an outline of what is said and done in the scene in which Bassanio makes choice of the caskets, from his entrance to the point where he is congratulated by his friends.

Honour Matriculation and Entrance into the Faculties of Education

1. (*a*) Show how Shakespeare brings out progressively in the Trial scene the evil of Shylock's nature, so that he should merit his punishment in the main.

(*b*) Show, by comparing the speeches of the three suitors, that the choice of the caskets is a test of character.

2. (*a*) Nerissa believed that the "lottery" of the caskets was a "good inspiration" of Portia's father. (i) State the conditions of the "lottery." (ii) What evidence is there in the play that her faith in the "inspiration" was justified?

(*b*) What is the dramatic purpose in *The Merchant of Venice* of (i) Antonio's melancholy, Act I., Scene 1; (ii) the arrival, immediately after Bassanio has chosen successfully, of Antonio's letter telling him that his "bond to the Jew is forfeit?"

(*c*) What are the two chief motives of Shylock? Do they ever conflict with each other? If so, which proves the stronger? Give references to support your answer in each case.

3. (*a*) What is the dramatic purpose of the speeches of the three suitors of Portia, made immediately before they choose? Support your answer by references to the speeches.

(*b*) "Shylock says the finest things in the play and he has the advantage in the argument throughout." Show, by references to the play, how far you think this statement is justified by the facts.

4. (*a*) What qualities in the character of Shylock are exhibited (i) in Act I., Scene 3, where Bassanio and Antonio come to borrow the money; (ii) in Act II., Scene 5, where Shylock tells Jessica he

is bid forth to supper; (iii) in Act III., Scene 1., where Shylock discovers the flight of his daughter?

(b) What are the merits of Portia's speech on *Mercy* that make it so widely known?

5. Give an estimate of the character of Bassanio as represented in *The Merchant of Venice*.

6. "That such a bond should be proposed, that when proposed it should be accepted, that it should be seriously entertained by a court of justice, that if entertained at all it should be upset on so frivolous a pretext as the omission of the reference to the shedding of blood; these form a series of impossible circumstances that any dramatist might despair of presenting with even an approach to naturalness."

State in a sentence or two in each case how Shakespeare succeeded in overcoming each of these difficulties in connection with the story of the pound of flesh in *The Merchant of Venice*.

7. Point out the various means whereby in *The Merchant of Venice* Shakespeare (a) evokes in the reader a measure of sympathy with Shylock, and (b) excites detestation of him.

8. (a) Refer to any indications of Portia's feelings with respect to each of the three suitors.

(b) State the important details of that portion of the scene following Bassanio's successful choice.

9. "Shylock is great in every scene where he appears, yet each later scene exhibits him in a new element or aspect of greatness."

By reference to the various scenes in which Shylock appears, estimate the truth of this statement.

10. (a) Show how the main stories of *The Merchant of Venice* are woven into a unity.

(b) What is contributed to this unified plot by the Lorenzo and Jessica story?

11. Show that the scene in *The Merchant of Venice*, in which Bassanio makes his choice, is the meeting place of the four stories in the play.

SUBJECTS FOR SHORT CLASS COMPOSITIONS

1. The Story of Jason (Act I., Scene I., ll. 175-8).

2. Why Shylock and Antonio are Enemies.

3. Bassanio's Former Visit to Belmont (his impressions of Portia; Portia's impressions of him).

4. The Bond (how it came that such a bond was ever proposed, and that Antonio was willing to sign it).

5. Bassanio and Antonio (Bassanio's past life; why he wishes to borrow of Antonio).

6. Morocco and Portia (the opinion each has of the other).

7. Bassanio's Plans, Preparations, and Departure.

8. The Masque (why it was held; who took part in it; the arrangements).

9. Shylock at Home.

10. Launcelot (why he left Shylock's service; why Bassanio employed him; how he was employed).

11. Jessica's Treatment of her Father.

12. The Elopement (how planned and how carried out).

13. The Prince of Arragon (Portia's opinion of him; why he chose the silver casket).

14. Tubal (who he is; the news he brings; his attitude towards Shylock).

15. Jessica's Elopement (its effect upon Shylock).

16. The Choice of the Caskets as a Test of Character.

17. Bassanio's Reasons for Choosing the Leaden Casket.

18. "The Casket Scene is the dramatic centre of the play."

19. Antonio's Fortunes (his wealth; his confidence; the news of his losses).

20. Portia's Plans to help Antonio (her arrangements regarding her house, her journey, her message to Bellario).

21. How Shylock Justifies his Treatment of Antonio.

22. Portia's Conduct of the Trial Scene.

23. Shylock's Punishment.

24. Lorenzo and Jessica (Tubal's story; why they came to Belmont).

25. The Rings' Story.

26. Gratiano (the part he plays in *The Merchant of Venice*).

STAGING A PLAY OF SHAKESPEARE

The plays of Shakespeare were written to be acted, and they are much more effective when put upon the stage than when merely read in class. In some schools, where there is a large staff and a large number of students and a good auditorium, it is possible to stage a complete play; and even in the smaller schools individual scenes may be put on with very little outlay for costume or scenery.

The simplest form of dramatic production consists merely in reading or reciting single scenes from a play of Shakespeare before the class, without special costumes or scenery, during the lesson period; and an occasional period spent in this way is a pleasing variation from the routine of class work. But needless to say, before any attempt is made to act scenes from the play in this way, they must be studied in class. The teacher, in this case, assigns the parts beforehand; the pupils learn the speeches and study how they should be spoken, and one or two practices are held after school hours to make the acting run smoothly. Sometimes two casts are chosen for the same scene, and it is a matter of rivalry to see which group of actors can produce the scene more effectively.

1

In schools where the teacher and pupils decide to stage a play in whole or in part for public performance, some sort of dramatic organization is required. If there is a dramatic club in the school it will naturally take full charge of the production; but, if not, the teacher and class must take the first steps to arrange for the play.

The first thing to be done is to select the play, and if possible it should be one that has been studied in class. The dramatic production should be the outgrowth of class work, and the would-be actor must make a study of the characters, the development of the plot, the structure of the play and the purpose of each scene. He must have studied the play so thoroughly that he knows the exact meaning of every expression, and is able to interpret the feelings of the various speakers in the play.

In any dramatic organization, the most important person is the director or stage-manager of the play, who is usually also the "coach", who gives instruction to the actors. The director has full charge of the production of the play, the rehearsals, the scenery and stage effects, the costumes, etc., etc. He must, of course, be assisted by various committees, but he directs their work and his decisions are in all cases final. He should not only have some knowledge of how to stage a play, but should have certain indispensable personal qualities such as tact, good humour, executive ability and decision. It is desirable, for obvious reasons, that some member of the staff should be the director of the school play; but experience and knowledge of stage production is the first consideration. The director, of course, does not himself take part in the play.

Next to the director, or stage-manager, the most important member of the organization is the "prompter", who is usually assistant stage-manager. He must be thoroughly familiar with the play, and in addition to his general services, it is his duty to prompt the actors at rehearsals and on the night of the performance.

The manager is assisted by a committee of students, each with specific duties. Different students, or committees of students, are given charge of:—

(a) The scenery, including the carpenter work and the curtain.

(b) The lighting, and electrical devices.

(c) The stage properties,—i.e. the furnishings and small articles—everything, in fact, except the costumes and scenery.

(d) The costumes.

(e) The music, including the orchestra.

(f) The make-up.

(g) The business details, advertising, printing, sale of tickets, ushers, etc.

It is necessary to guard against over-organization and over-lapping; and the director must use his discretion as to how many assistants are required.

In general, a play of Shakespeare is much too long for presentation on a modern stage, and even in single scenes certain parts may be cut out to advantage. The play must be studied carefully by the director, either with or without the class, in order to decide what scenes may be omitted and how the speeches may be shortened. As a result of this revision, an acting edition of the play is produced. It is better if possible, to give to each actor a typewritten copy of his own part in the play, rather than have him rely on the text as a whole.

One of the first duties of the director is to choose a cast for the play, and in making the selection he may be assisted by a committee of two or three judges. At the "try-out," those who wish to take part in the play are required to read a scene, or part of a scene, which they have prepared. In assigning parts to different students, the judges must take into account (a) the voice,—its carrying power, tone, flexibility, etc. (b) ability of the actor to enter into the spirit of the play, to *feel* the part he acts, and (c) his physical suitability for the part. No student should accept a part in the play unless he can give an assurance that he will attend the rehearsals faithfully and punctually. There should be a definite understanding on this point before the cast is completed.

Usually at least twelve or fifteen rehearsals are required, that is about three a week for five or six weeks. The first two or three rehearsals are given over to blocking out the action. The actors read their parts, and the director gives instructions as to entrances, exits, movements, acting, and stage "business." At these rehearsals no attention is paid to the speaker's voice or expression, but the actors must become familiar with their positions and movements on the stage, and the same routine must be followed at subsequent rehearsals. After this preliminary work has been done, the play must be studied scene by scene and line by line for the purpose of securing the proper interpretation and expression. The first Act is rehearsed repeatedly before proceeding with the second. When the acting and the reading go hand in hand, the actors learn their lines with little effort, and at the end of the first week, Act I should be letter-perfect. It is not always necessary to have the full cast present at the rehearsals, for single speeches and single scenes may sometimes be rehearsed to better advantage when only those immediately concerned are present. During the week immediately preceding the final performance, rehearsals are held every evening, and the "dress" rehearsals on the last two or three evenings should be held in the hall or theatre where the play is to be acted.

It is impossible within the limits of a few pages, to give detailed instructions regarding staging and acting; but there are one or two general directions which it is well for the actors to keep in mind:

For those who are taking part in the play the all-important thing is that they should *feel* the parts that they are acting. The actor who loses himself in his part is scarcely conscious of his audience, and he has no temptation to declaim. He speaks naturally, usually in a conversational tone, and he gives free expression to his emotions. "Did you see Kean in Othello?" some one asked Kemble. "No," replied Kemble, "I did not see Mr. Kean. I saw Othello." The student who enters so completely into the play that he forgets himself in the part that he is acting is likely, on the whole, to prove a better actor than the student who merely recites his lines. His speech is less hurried; his acting is more natural; he does not make unnecessary movements, and he does not let his eyes wander from the stage to the audience. He must, however, always bear in mind that his speech must be heard by the audience. This necessitates clear enunciation and proper voice-control; and the actor must always occupy a position on the stage that will enable the audience to hear him.

On the mechanical side, in staging a play it is safer for the amateur to err on the side of simplicity rather than make his production too elaborate. The scenery and the stage-furnishings should be of the simplest. Most of the text-books on dramatics give directions for making stage settings of plain and cheap materials. In modern play-production, footlights and spotlights are sparingly used, and the stage is lighted from the wings and from above. Most amateur producers are troubled as to "make-up"; but for most plays very little make-up is required,—only enough to prevent the face from appearing too pale. But for these and all other details relating to the staging of the play, the stage-manager may be relied upon, and there are many books on dramatics which may be consulted by the amateur.

The following are a few of the well-known books on the subject:

Shakespeare for Community Players by Roy Mitchell. J. M. Dent and Sons, Toronto.

Practical Stage-Directing for Amateurs, by Emerson Taylor. E. P. Dutton & Co., New York.

How to Produce Amateur Plays, by Barrett H. Clark. Little, Brown & Co., Boston.

Producing in Little Theatres, by Clarence Stratton. Henry Holt & Co., New York.

Book for Shakespeare Plays and Pageants, by O. L. Hatcher. E. P. Dutton & Co., New York.

Play Production for Amateurs, by F. H. Koch. University of North Carolina Extension Bulletin.